A. E. HOUSMAN

SELECTED PROSE

A. E. HOUSMAN
SELECTED PROSE

EDITED BY
JOHN CARTER

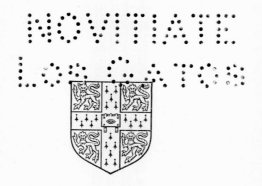

NOVITIATE
LOS GATOS

CAMBRIDGE
AT THE UNIVERSITY PRESS
1962

PUBLISHED BY
THE SYNDICS OF THE CAMBRIDGE UNIVERSITY PRESS

Bentley House, 200 Euston Road, London, N.W. 1
American Branch: 32 East 57th Street, New York 22, N.Y.
West African Office: P.O. Box 33, Ibadan, Nigeria

©

CAMBRIDGE UNIVERSITY PRESS
1961

First edition   1961
Reprinted with corrections 1962

Printed in Great Britain at the University Press, Cambridge
(Brooke Crutchley, University Printer)

CONTENTS

PREFACE

Much has been written about Housman since his death in 1936. We have had reminiscences, and appreciations, and critiques: from his sister Mrs E. W. Symons, from A. W. Pollard and Mr Alan Ker, from Professors R. W. Chambers, G. B. A. Fletcher, F. W. Oliver and O. L. Richmond, from Miss Joan Thompson, Mr Cyril Connolly, and Mr John Sparrow, to look no farther than his own country.[1] His brother Laurence's official memoir appeared in 1937,[2] and it was followed in 1940 by Dr Percy Withers's sympathetic volume of personal recollections, *A Buried Life*. In 1941 Grant Richards, Housman's publisher since 1898 and his familiar friend, produced a long biography[3] enlivened (as is Laurence Housman's) by numerous quotations from letters, and exceptional among the source-books as showing its subject in his more relaxed moods. (Housman wrote very good letters, always in his own hand and never to my knowledge on headed paper: if they could be collected, they would repay the trouble.) In 1957 Mr George L. Watson, in *A. E. Housman: A Divided Life*, delved farther than his predecessors into the thorny question of those 'great and real troubles of my early life', the causes of that 'continuous excitement' under which (its author has told us) most of *A Shropshire Lad* was written in 1895. And in 1958 Mr Norman Marlow, of Manchester University, gave us *A. E. Housman: Scholar and Poet*. Meanwhile, hardly a month can have passed since 1936 without an article or a note, the discovery of an echo or the adducing of a parallel, being printed in one of the learned or less learned periodicals, especially in the United States.

Yet (if readers of the *Introductory Lecture*[4] will allow me the paraphrase) when it comes to a true appreciation of Housman, heap up in one scale all those hundreds of pages, and drop into the other the thin green volume of Mr Gow's *Sketch* of 1936,[5] and the first scale, as Milton says, will straight fly up and kick the beam.

The majority of posthumous attention has been about evenly divided between the small body of Housman's poetry and the large 'enigma' of his personality, with neither of which we are here concerned. Outside Mr Gow's authoritative and judicious pages, comment on his scholarship, which was avowedly by far the most important element in his life, has been sparse and somewhat muted. This is understandable. When, in his lifetime, someone wrote of him as the first scholar in Europe, Housman said 'It is not true, and if it were, —— would not know it'. And such was his eventual ascendancy that today, after a quarter of a century, the scholar who took up his pen to essay a comparison between Housman and, say, Porson or Wilamowitz would be likely to put it down again quickly for fear of provoking, if only in imagination, one of those blistering comments for which the editor of Manilius was notorious.

Whether or not it was Housman's failure in Greats at Oxford in 1881 (he did not merely fail to get a first: he was actually ploughed) that inspired—or if it did not inspire, steeled—his resolve to build himself a monument in the narrow world of exact scholarship, the performance of the ensuing eleven years was phenomenal. His free evenings from a clerkship in the Patent Office were spent in the British Museum. The fruit of these, and perhaps also of his 'misspent' days at Oxford, appeared in profusion in the learned journals between 1888 and 1891. Such was

its quality and impact that when Housman stood for the
Latin chair at University College London in the following
year, the candidature of this obscure young man, whose
application proclaimed his failure at Oxford and who had
never held a university post of even the humblest kind, was
endorsed in the most respectful terms by fifteen of the
foremost scholars of the day: among them the Professors of
Latin at Oxford, Cambridge and Dublin, the Professors
of Greek at Dublin and St Andrews, and those two
Cambridge paragons, A. W. Verrall and Henry Jackson;
not to mention Gildersleeve from America and Wecklein
from Germany. 'Mr Housman's position is in the very
first rank of scholars and critics', wrote Arthur Palmer;
'I regard him', said Tyrrell, 'as holding a place in the very
van of modern scholarship'; Nettleship considered that
'his peculiar gifts...deserve, in an especial way, public
recognition in England'; 'I can say without hesitation',
wrote Verrall, 'that there is no one for whose judgment
I have more respect.' Perhaps only those conversant with
the trades-unionism of Academe can appreciate to the full
the exceptional character of such a volley of endorsements.

It would be an hyperbole to say that Housman emerged,
like Athene from the head of Zeus, fully armed. Yet
even his early papers show a penetration, a command of
the weapons of scholarship, a power, very remarkable in
a man just turning thirty. And even those of us who are
not equipped to judge of the scholarship can feel, before the
turn of the century, the weight of authority which carried
Housman from London to the chair of Latin at Cambridge
in 1911. A quarter of a century later, in an obituary notice
in the *Classical Review*, Professor D. S. Robertson summed
up thus:

Housman's excellence as a scholar was perhaps chiefly due to his
simultaneous possession of so many different qualities. His alertness

in scenting corruption, the dexterity of his remedies, and the sharpness
of his wit are obvious to every reader, and almost equally obvious,
though he kept it in the background, is the sureness of his aesthetic
judgment, but it is sometimes forgotten that behind this arresting
brilliance lay patience which shrank from no drudgery, memory which
let nothing slip, and absolute honesty in the pursuit of truth.

The proper appreciation of these last qualities is
inevitably restricted to professional scholars. Their bare
results, as marshalled in the austere pages of the learned
journals and in the major part of the prefaces to Manilius,
Juvenal and Lucan, are stiff going even for those with a
good understanding of Latin and Greek. The ordinary
reader, with a smattering of either or both, can join the
experts only when Housman moves from illustration to
conclusion, from argument to the statement of principle,
from analysis of an editor's work to an estimate of his
capacity. It is our good fortune that Latin, as the *lingua
franca* of classical scholarship, had by 1900 yielded to
the vernacular, at least for prefaces and reviews. For
Housman, as it is the objective of this book to demonstrate,
was just as much an artist in prose as he was in verse.

This has of course been apparent, even to those who do
not normally read the classical authors and their commentators, since *The Name and Nature of Poetry* was published
in 1933 and the *Introductory Lecture* (of 1892) in 1937.[6]
Housman himself, in later life, described the latter as
'rhetorical and not wholly sincere'. Much of the interest of
the former (which was his latest, as the other was his earliest,
substantial piece of prose composition to survive) lay in
the very candour of its sincerity; and even Housman's
severest critic (himself) could not have called it rhetorical.
If it seems, by comparison, easy and informal in style,
we remember the words he used in declining the office of
Public Orator at Cambridge: 'You none of you know...
what a trouble composition is to me (in prose, I mean:

poetry is either easy or impossible). When the job is done, it may have a certain amount of form and finish and perhaps a false air of ease; but there is an awful history behind it.' Housman was thinking, Mr Gow tells us,[7] of more formal compositions; 'but what he said was true even of his learned work. The wit which flashes out here and there in his controversial writings, and blazes with sustained brilliance through pages of the prefaces to Manilius and Juvenal, was no spontaneous outpouring but, as was evident from his papers, the result of careful labour.'

It is perhaps partly the fact that much of Housman's prose has had to be ferreted out of the learned journals or procured from the secondhand booksellers which has inhibited most of the biographers and commentators from paying it as much attention as it deserves. Yet if a little effort is required to follow all the signposts provided by Mr Gow's list of Housman's writings, the preface to Manilius, Book I, at least, has long been cherished by amateurs of invective. In 1904 the few paragraphs devoted to this major work of textual scholarship among the *Classical Review*'s 'Briefer Notices' included the dry observation that the preface is written 'in the slashing style which all know and few applaud'. In 1930 Housman's preface to Book v opens with the following paragraph:

The first volume of the edition of Manilius now completed was published in 1903, the second in 1912, the third in 1916, and the fourth in 1920. All were produced at my own expense and offered to the public at much less than cost price; but this unscrupulous artifice did not overcome the natural disrelish of mankind for the combination of a tedious author with an odious editor. Of each volume there were printed 400 copies: only the first is yet sold out, and that took 23 years; and the reason why it took no longer is that it found purchasers among the unlearned, who had heard that it contained a scurrilous preface and hoped to extract from it a low enjoyment.

There can be no doubt, I think, that Housman relished his
own skill with the rapier and the scalpel, even sometimes
with the knuckle-duster. The majority of his readers have
relished it too, and an anthologist of polemical savagery
(turning satiated from Bentley's *Dissertation on the Epistles
of Phalaris* or Porson's *Letters to Travis*) would find many
a plum among Housman's classical papers to match the
numerous specimens quoted by Mr Gow. I have my own
favourites among the less familiar: for example, 'works of
this sort are little better than interruptions to our studies',
or 'all the tools he uses are two-edged, though to be sure
both edges are quite blunt', or 'his main purpose in
withholding indispensable information and deceiving the
reader by silence is to find room for a long record of
conjectures which dishonour the human intellect'. But
in making the selection here offered I have done my best
to resist the obvious temptation. I have chosen, in those
sections (II and III, particularly the latter) where extracts
had to be made, passages or paragraphs which seem to
me both representative expressions of Housman's stance as
a scholar and critic and also characteristic examples of his
powers as a prose stylist. The fact that he is found occupied
more often with censure and refutation than with praise
is in the nature of the material. As he himself once said:
'I have spent most of my time in finding faults because
finding faults, if they are real and not imaginary, is the
most useful sort of criticism.'

Yet if Housman was (as indeed he was) an unsparing
critic of the scholarship of others, no man was better
equipped to assess the comparative merits of his predecessors,
or more judicious in his appreciations of them. Few men
have been as well versed in the history of post-Renais-
sance classical scholarship. He was punctilious, and con-
sciously so because others commonly were not, in attribut-

ing emendations or interpretations to their original
begetters, no matter how recondite the work in which they
appeared. He seems to have read everything written by
anybody, however humdrum, about any classical author,
however obscure. And if Bentley was his hero ('Bentley is
alone and supreme', 'Bentley would cut up into four of
me'), with H. A. J. Munro perhaps the most admired of
his near-contemporaries, the extracts printed here provide
many a sample of Housman's intimate familiarity with the
work of Scaliger and Heinsius and Gronovius, of Dawes,
Markland and Elmsley, of Lachmann and Madvig and
Baehrens, and (more important) of the nicety of his judgment of their capacities and the even-handedness of its
expression.

I must forestall the objections of the learned minority by
explaining that, in the interest of the unlearned majority, I
have not hesitated here and there to omit (with the conventional asterisks) pockets of Latin and Greek, cited as
examples or for supporting evidence. Scholars can supply
the omissions by going to the source (indicated, if they
do not know it, in the notes), while the layman may judge
what a full-dress Housman review looks like—I had almost
written, feels like—from an example printed in full at p. 72.

As to the arrangement: the two lectures place themselves,
by content as well as by date, at the beginning and at the
end (Housman's inaugural lecture as Professor of Latin at
Cambridge in 1911 has never been printed, nor does the
manuscript survive). The selections from the Prefaces (II)
are followed by selections from reviews, etc. These are
printed in chronological order, with those of English books
forming, as it happens, a group at the end; and this section
(III) concludes with a couple of examples of Housman's
letters to the press. The 1921 address to the Classical

Association (IV) is a summary exposition, dating from
the year before *Last Poems* was published, of the principles of textual criticism exemplified in the preceding
sections.

After this comes a pair of biographical pieces, of which
the more considerable was written as preface to a posthumous collection of the essays of Arthur Platt, Professor
of Greek at University College London from 1894 to 1924
and Housman's closest friend among his colleagues there.
Deeply touched with affection, this has a place of its own in
his published work; and it contains one passage which
must seem especially significant to those of us who regret
that Housman devoted so much of his first-rate talent to
the editing of second-rate authors. Of Platt's studies he
writes, after generous commendation, that they were not
'warped and narrowed by ambition. A scholar [he explains]
who means to build himself a monument must spend much
of his life in acquiring knowledge which for its own sake
is not worth having and in reading books which in themselves do not deserve to be read; *at illa iacent multa et
praeclara relicta.*' Surely we can hear the sigh under the
breath: Platt built no monument, but he had a happy
life.

The penultimate section contains the identified examples
(all originally anonymous) of Housman's skill as a com-
poser of ceremonial pieces. That he was chosen as official
lapidarist by a college, and later by a university, by no
means ill-furnished with accomplished writers is testimony
to Cambridge's judgment of the Kennedy Professor of
Latin's command of English prose; and if these are by
their nature compositional exercises, we shall agree, I
think, that Cambridge's confidence was not misplaced.

The content of the appendix demands a word of justification. Mr Gow has recorded that Housman was com-

plaisant in obliging the University College Literary Society
with papers on a number of English poets.

In their kind [he writes],[8] they were excellent; they would not have
enhanced his reputation but they would not have impaired it, and it is
to be regretted that he refused an invitation from the Cambridge
University Press to publish them, and gave his executors instructions
that they were to be destroyed.

A friend once expressed to Housman the hope that the paper on
Swinburne might be published, and, on hearing that it was to be
destroyed after his death, ventured to suggest that if Housman
thought it bad he would already have destroyed it himself. 'I do not
think it bad,' said Housman; 'I think it not good enough for me';
and his precautions that these papers, which he considered πάρεργα,
should not survive are characteristic.

Despite the precautions, however, some part (exordium?
peroration?) of one of them did survive: in a typescript
copy among the papers devotedly preserved by his sister,
Mrs Symons. It deals with Matthew Arnold, for whose
writings Housman had a profound respect. I am quite sure
that its author, and reasonably sure that Mr Gow, will not
approve of its being printed here. But here it is.

I am indebted to Mr Ronald Mansbridge, to the Syndics
of the University Press, and to the present owner of the
Housman copyrights for the invitation to do something I
have wanted to do for twenty years; to Mr John Sparrow,
long my companion and ever my mentor in Housmanian
studies, for his encouragement and advice; and to the late
Laurence Haward, whose comprehensive assemblage of
Housman's contributions to the learned journals (putting
my own modest collection to shame) is now in the library
of King's College, Cambridge, as pleasant a place to work
in as I know.

JOHN CARTER

'It was impossible to listen attentively to Housman for long without becoming aware that one was in contact with a mind of extraordinary distinction; and it is not only, or even chiefly, to professional scholars that such a contact is fascinating and exhilarating.'

A. S. F. Gow, *A. E. Housman*, p. 44.

I

INTRODUCTORY
LECTURE

This introductory lecture was delivered before the Faculties of Arts and Laws and of Science in University College London, on 3 October 1892. The prefatory Note by Mr Gow to the first published edition, 1937, reads as follows: 'It was the custom at University College, London, to open the academic year with a lecture to the united Faculties of the College, delivered by a Professor, and most commonly by one who had recently joined the staff. In October 1892 Housman, then in his thirty-fourth year, was about to take up his duties as Professor of Latin, and the lecture, though not technically his inaugural address, was his first pronouncement from the Latin Chair. It has not previously been published, but it was printed privately in 1892 for the College, and again in 1933 for Mr John Carter and Mr John Sparrow, on both occasions by the present publishers. Long afterwards Housman described it as "rhetorical and not wholly sincere", but nobody familiar with his work can doubt the sincerity of its central theme, the value of learning for its own sake; and Housman himself sanctioned the reprint in 1933, desiring only to have it stated that "the Council of University College, not I, had the lecture printed. I consented, because it seemed churlish to refuse. This is the purport of nescit vox missa reverti" [printed on the title-page]. *Housman's seems to have been the only Introductory Lecture so honoured by the Council.*

* 'The text of this edition [and of the present one] is that of the 1933 reprint, in which Housman made one correction.'*

EVERY exercise of our faculties, says Aristotle, has some good for its aim; and if he speaks true it becomes a matter of importance that when we exert any special faculty we should clearly apprehend the special good at which we are aiming. What now is the good which we set before us as our end when we exercise our faculties in acquiring knowledge, in learning? The answers differ, and they differ for this reason,—that people seldom approach the question impartially, but usually bring with them a prepossession in favour of this or that department of knowledge. Everyone has his favourite study, and he is therefore disposed to lay down, as the aim of learning in general, the aim which his favourite study seems specially fitted to achieve, and the recognition of which as the aim of learning in general would increase the popularity of that study and the importance of those who profess it. This method, conclusion first, reasons afterwards, has always been in high favour with the human race: you write down at the outset the answer to the sum; then you proceed to fabricate, not for use but for exhibition to the public, the ciphering by which you can pretend to have arrived at it. The method has one obvious advantage,—that you are thus quite sure of reaching the conclusion you want to reach: if you began with your reasons there is no telling where they might lead you, and like enough you would never get to the desired conclusion at all. But it has one drawback,—that unanimity is thus unattainable: every man gives the answer which seems right in his own eyes. And accordingly we find that the aim of acquiring knowledge is differently defined by different people. In how many different ways, I do not know; but it will be sufficient for today to consider the answers given by two great parties: the advocates of those sciences which have now succeeded in arrogating to themselves the name of Science, and of those studies which call themselves by the title, perhaps equally arrogant, of Humane Letters.

The partisans of Science define the aim of learning to be utility. I do not mean to say that any eminent man of science commits himself to this opinion: some of them have publicly and scornfully repudiated it, and all of them, I imagine, reject it in their hearts. But there is no denying that this is the view which makes Science popular; this is the impression under which the British merchant or manufacturer dies and leaves his money to endow scientific education. And since this impression, though false, is nevertheless beneficent in its results, those who are inter- ested in scientific pursuits may very well consider that it is no business of theirs to dispel a delusion which promises so well for the world in general and for themselves in particular. The popular view, I say, is that the aim of acquiring knowledge is to equip one's self for the business of life; that accordingly the knowledge most to be sought after is the knowledge which equips one best; and that this knowledge is Science. And the popular view has the very distinguished countenance of Mr Herbert Spencer. Mr Spencer, in his well-known treatise on Education, pro- nounces that education to be of most value which prepares us for self-preservation by preparing us for securing the necessaries of life; and that is education in the sciences. 'For,' says he, 'leaving out only some very small classes, what are all men employed in? They are employed in the production, preparation and distribution of commodities. And on what does efficiency in the production, preparation and distribution of commodities depend? It depends on the use of methods fitted to the respective natures of these commodities; it depends on an adequate acquaintance with their physical, chemical and vital properties, as the case may be; that is, it depends on Science.' And then he proceeds with his usual exactness of detail to shew in what way each several science serves to render one efficient in producing, preparing or distributing commodities.

Now to begin with, it is evident that if we are to pursue Science simply in order to obtain an adequate acquaintance with the physical, chemical and vital properties of the commodities which we produce, prepare or distribute, we shall not need to pursue Science far. Mr Spencer duly rehearses the list of the sciences, and is at much pains to demonstrate the bearing of each science on the arts of life. Take one for a specimen. I suppose that in no science have Englishmen more distinguished themselves than in astronomy: one need but mention the name of Isaac Newton. And it is a science which has not only fascinated the profoundest intellects but has always laid a strong hold on the popular imagination, so that, for example, our newspapers found it paid them to fill a good deal of space with articles about the present apposition of the planet Mars. And now listen to the reasons why we are to study astronomy. 'Of the concrete sciences we come first to Astronomy. Out of this has grown that art of navigation which has made possible the enormous foreign commerce that supports a large part of our population, while supplying us with many necessaries and most of our luxuries.' That is all there is to say about astronomy: that navigation has grown out of it. Well then, we want no Isaac Newtons; let them carry their Principias to another market. Astronomy is a squeezed orange as far as we are concerned. Astronomers may transfer their residence to the remotest world they can discover, and welcome, for all the need we have of them here: the enormous foreign commerce which Mr Spencer speaks of will still enable this island to be over-populated, and our currants and cocoanuts will continue to arrive with their former regularity. Hundreds

and hundreds of years ago astronomy had reached the
point which satisfies our modest requirements: it had
given birth to navigation. They were conversing in Athens
four centuries before Christ, and a young Spencerian
named Glaucon already found more than this to say in
praise of the utility of astronomy. 'Shall we make astronomy one of our studies,' asked Socrates,'or do you dissent?'
'No, I agree,' said Glaucon, 'for to have an intimate
acquaintance with seasons, and months, and years, is an
advantage not only to the farmer and the navigator, but
also, in an equal degree, to the general,'—an aspect of
astronomical science which appears to have escaped
Mr Spencer's notice.

Astronomy, you may say, is not a fair example to take,
because of all sciences it is perhaps the one which least
concerns the arts of life. May be; but this difference
between astronomy and other sciences is a difference of
degree alone. Just as even astronomy, though it touches
practical life but little, does nevertheless touch it, so those
sciences, such as chemistry and physics, which are the
most intimately and widely concerned with practical
life, nevertheless throughout a great portion of their
range have no contact with it at all. If it is in order to
secure the necessaries of life that we are to study chemistry
and physics, we shall study them further no doubt than we
shall for that reason study astronomy, but not so far by
a long way as chemists and physicists do in fact study them
now. Electric lighting and aniline dyes and other such
magnificent alleviations of human destiny do not spring
into being at every forward step in our knowledge of the
physical forces and chemical composition of the universe:
they are merely occasional incidents, flowers by the way.
Much in both sciences which the chemist and the physicist
study with intense interest and delight will be set aside as

curious and unprofitable learning by our producer, pre-
parer or distributor of commodities. In short, the fact is,
that what man will seek to acquaint himself with in order
to prepare him for securing the necessaries of life is not
Science, but the indispensable minimum of Science.

And just as our knowledge of Science need not be deep,
so too it need not be wide. Mr Spencer shews that every
science is of some use to some man or another. But not
every science is of use to every man. Geometry, he points
out, is useful to the carpenter, and chemistry to the calico-
printer. True; but geometry is not useful to the calico-
printer, nor chemistry to the carpenter. If it is to secure
the necessaries of life that men pursue Science, the sciences
that each man needs to pursue are few. In addition to the
initial studies of reading, writing and arithmetic, he needs
to acquaint himself with those sciences, or rather, as I said
before, with the indispensable minimum of those sciences,
which concern the trade or the art he earns his bread by:
the dyer with chemistry, the carpenter with geometry,
the navigator with astronomy. But there he can stop.
Mr Spencer appears to apprehend this; and since such
a result is far from his desires, he attempts, in the case of
one or two sciences, to shew that no one can neglect them
with impunity. The following, for instance, is the method
by which he endeavours to terrorise us into studying
geology. We may, any of us, some day, take shares in a
joint-stock company; and that company may engage in
mining operations; and those operations may be directed
to the discovery of coal; and for want of geological information the joint-stock company may go mining for
coal under the old red sandstone, where there is no coal;
and then the mining operations will be fruitless, and the
joint-stock company will come to grief, and where shall
we be then? This is, indeed, to eat the bread of carefulness.

After all, men have been known to complete their pilgrimage through this vale of tears without taking shares in a joint-stock company. But the true reply to Mr Spencer's intimidations I imagine to be this: that the attempt to fortify man's estate against all contingencies by such precautions as these is in the first place interminable and in the second place hopeless. As Sarpedon says to Glaucus in the *Iliad*, a hundred thousand fates stand close to us always, which none can flee and none avoid. The complexity of the universe is infinite, and the days of a man's life are threescore years and ten. One lifetime, nine lifetimes are not long enough for the task of blocking every cranny through which calamity may enter. And say that we could thus triumphantly succeed in the attempt at self-preservation; say that we could thus impregnably secure the necessaries of existence; even then the true business of life is not so much as begun. Existence is not itself a good thing, that we should spend a lifetime securing its necessaries: a life spent, however victoriously, in securing the necessaries of life is no more than an elaborate furnishing and decoration of apartments for the reception of a guest who is never to come. Our business here is not to live, but to live happily. We may seem to be occupied, as Mr Spencer says, in the production, preparation and distribution of commodities; but our true occupation is to manufacture from the raw material of life the fabric of happiness; and if we are ever to set about our work we must make up our minds to risk something. Absolute security for existence is unattainable, and no wise man will pursue it; for if we must go to these lengths in the attempt at self-preservation we shall die before ever we have begun to live. Reasonable security is attainable; but it is attainable without any wide study of Science.

And if we grant for the moment that to secure the

necessaries of life is the true aim of Science, and if we also grant, as we well may, that Science is really of some use in compassing that aim, still it is apparent that other things compass it much more effectually than Science. It is not found in experience that men of science are those who make the largest fortunes out of the production, preparation and distribution of commodities. The men who have risen, if you can call it rising, from barge-boys to millionaires, have not risen by their knowledge of science. They have sometimes risen by other people's knowledge of science, but their own contribution to their success, so far as it consists in knowledge at all, consists rather in their knowledge of business and their knowledge of men. Therefore, to sum up, when we find that for purposes of practical utility we need no wide knowledge of the sciences and no deep knowledge of any science, and that even for these purposes Science is not the most serviceable sort of knowledge, surely we are justified in concluding that the true aim of Science is something other than utility.

While the partisans of Science define the end of education as the useful, the partisans of the Humanities define it, more sublimely, as the good and the beautiful. We study, they say, not that we may earn a livelihood, but that we may transform and beautify our inner nature by culture. Therefore the true and the really valuable knowledge is that which is properly and distinctively human; the knowledge, as Matthew Arnold used to call it, of the best which has been said and thought in the world,—the literature which contains the history of the spirit of man.

Here indeed is an aim which no one will pretend to despise. The names of the good and the beautiful are treated with respect even by those who give themselves little trouble about the things; and if the study of the Humanities will really transform and beautify our inner

nature, it will be acknowledged that so soon as we have
acquired, with all possible despatch, that minimum of
scientific knowledge which is necessary to put our material
welfare in a state of reasonable security, we ought to apply
ourselves earnestly and long to the study of the Humanities.
And as a man should always magnify his own office,
nothing could be more natural or agreeable to me than to
embrace this opinion and to deliver here a panegyric of the
Humanities and especially of that study on which the
Humanities are founded, the study of the dead languages of
Greece and Rome. I am deterred from doing so, in the first
place, because it is possible that a partisan harangue of that
sort might not be relished by the united Faculties of Arts,
Laws and Science; and secondly because to tell the truth
I do not much believe in these supposed effects of classical
studies. I do not believe that the proportion of the human
race whose inner nature the study of the classics will specially transform and beautify is large; and I am quite sure
that the proportion of the human race on whom the classics
will confer that benefit can attain the desired end without
that minute and accurate study of the classical tongues
which affords Latin professors their only excuse for existing.

How shall we judge whether a man's nature has been
transformed and beautified? and where will the transformation and beautification begin? I never yet heard it
maintained by the wildest enthusiast for Classics that the
standard of morality or even of amiability is higher among
classical scholars than among men of Science. The special
benefit which these studies are supposed, and in some cases
justly supposed, to confer, is to quicken our appreciation
of what is excellent and to refine our discrimination between what is excellent and what is not. And since
literature is the instrument by which this education is
imparted, it is in the domain of literature that this

quickened appreciation and sharpened discrimination ought first to display themselves. And so in fact they do. If anyone wants convincing of the inestimable value of a classical education to those who are naturally qualified to profit by it, let him compare our two greatest poets, Shakespeare and Milton, and see what the classics did for one and what the lack of the classics did for the other. Milton was steeped through and through with classical literature; and he is the one English poet from whom an Englishman ignorant of Greek and Latin can learn what the great classics were like. Mark: the classics cannot be said to have succeeded altogether in transforming and beautifying Milton's inner nature. They did not sweeten his naturally disagreeable temper; they did not enable him to conduct controversy with urbanity or even with decency. But in the province of literature, where their influence is soonest and most powerfully exerted, they conferred on him all the benefits which their encomiasts ascribe to them. The dignity, the sanity, the unfaltering elevation of style, the just subordination of detail, the due adaptation of means to ends, the high respect of the crafts-man for his craft and for himself, which ennoble Virgil and the great Greeks, are all to be found in Milton, and nowhere else in English literature are they all to be found: certainly not in Shakespeare. In richness of natural endowment Shakespeare was the superior even of Milton; but he had small Latin and less Greek, and the result—I do not know that Samuel Johnson states the result too harshly when he has the noble courage to say that Shakespeare has nowhere written more than six consecutive lines of good poetry. It is told in a Christian legend that when St Paul was in Italy he was led to Virgil's grave at Parthenope, and that he wept over it and said 'O Chief of poets, what would not I have made of thee, had I but found thee living!'

Ad Maronis mausoleum
Ductus, fudit super eum
Piae rorem lacrimae:
'Quem te' inquit 'reddidissem,
Si te vivum invenissem,
Poetarum maxime!'

I can imagine Virgil himself, in the year 1616, when he welcomed Shakespeare to the Elysian fields, I can imagine Virgil weeping and saying,

'Quem te reddidissem,
Si te vivum invenissem,
Poetarum maxime!'

Virgil and the Greeks would have made Shakespeare not merely a great genius, which he was already, but, like Milton, a great artist, which he is not. He would have gained from the classics that virtue in which he and all his contemporaries are so wofully deficient, sobriety. He would have learnt to discriminate between what is permanently attractive and what is merely fashionable or popular. And perhaps it is not too much to hope that with the example of the classics before him he would have developed a literary conscience and taken a pride in doing his best, instead of scamping his work because he knew his audience would never find out how ill he was writing. But it was not to be; and there is only too much justice in the exclamation of that eminent Shakespearian critic King George III, 'Was there ever such stuff as great part of Shakespeare?' Shakespeare, who at his best is the best of all poets, at his worst is almost the worst. I take a specimen not from any youthful performance but from one of his maturest works, a play which contains perhaps the most beautiful poetry that even Shakespeare ever wrote, *The Winter's Tale*. He desires to say that a lady shed tears; and thus he says it: 'Her eyes became two spouts.'

That was the sort of atrocity the Elizabethan audience liked, and Shakespeare gave it them to their hearts' content: sometimes, no doubt, with the full knowledge that it was detestable; sometimes, I greatly fear, in good faith, because he had no worthy model to guide him.

The classics, I say, must have done for Shakespeare what they did for Milton; but what proportion of mankind are even accessible to this influence? What proportion offer even a foothold for the entrance of literary culture into their minds? The classics can indeed quicken our appreciation of what is excellent; but can they implant it? They can refine our discrimination between good and bad; but can they create it? Take the greatest scholar that England or perhaps that Europe ever bred; a man so great that in his own province he serves for a touchstone of merit and has always been admired by all admirable scholars and despised by all despicable scholars: Richard Bentley. Bentley was born in the year 1662, and he brought with him into the world, like most men born near that date, a prosaic mind; nor did all his immense study of the classics avail to confer on him a true appreciation of poetry. While he dealt with the classical poets he was comparatively safe, for in dealing with these a prosaic mind is not so grave a disqualification as a dithyrambic mind; and Bentley had lived with the ancients till he understood them as no one will ever understand them who brings to their study a taste formed on the poetry of Elizabeth's time or ours. But that jealous deity which loves, Herodotus tells us, to strike down towering things, put it into his heart to invade a literature with which he was ill acquainted, and to edit *Paradise Lost*. He persuaded himself that Milton in his blindness had become the victim of an unscrupulous person, who had introduced into the poem a great deal that Milton never wrote, and had altered for the worse a

great deal that he did write. Accordingly, whenever
Milton's poetry failed to come up to Bentley's prosaic
notions of what poetry ought to be, he detected the hand,
or, as he preferred to call it, the fist, of this first editor.
Milton relates how 'four speedy Cherubim' were sent out
with trumpets to summon an assembly. 'Four *speedy*
Cherubim' says Bentley: 'Not much need of swiftness to
be a good trumpeter. For *speedy* I suspect the poet gave
"Four *sturdy* Cherubim." Stout, robust, able to blow a
strong blast.' Milton relates how Uriel at sunset came to
Paradise to warn the guards of the approach of Satan:
'Thither came Uriel, gliding through the even.' Bentley
insists on altering *even* to *heaven*, because, as he acutely
observes, evening is a division of time, not of space, and
consequently you cannot come gliding through it: you
might as well say, he exclaims, 'came gliding through
six o'clock.' Milton relates how Ithuriel found Satan
disguised as a toad whispering at the ear of Eve: 'Him,
thus intent, Ithuriel with his spear Touched lightly.'
But Bentley cannot be happy without Ithuriel's motive
for doing so, and accordingly inserts a verse of his own
composition: 'Him, thus intent, Ithuriel with his spear,
Knowing no real toad durst there intrude, Touched lightly.'
Here was a man of true and even colossal genius, yet you
see in matters poetical the profoundest knowledge of the
classics profited him nothing, because he had been born
without the organs by which poetical excellence is perceived. And so are most men born without them; and the
quickening and refining influences special to literature run
off them like water off a duck's back. It is the magnet and
the churn in the song: 'If I can wheedle a knife or a
needle, Why not a silver churn?' quoth the magnet; but
he found his mistake; and where literature is the magnet
most men are silver churns. It is nothing to be ashamed of,

though on the other hand it is not much to be conceited about, as some people seem to think it. Different men have different aptitudes, and this aptitude happens to be uncommon; and the majority, not only of other men, but the majority also of professed students of the classics, whatever else they may get from those studies, do not get from them a just appreciation of literary excellence. True, we are not all so easily found out as Bentley, because we have not Bentley's intrepid candour. There is a sort of savage nobility about his firm reliance on his own bad taste: we on the other hand usually fit our judgments not to the truth of things nor even to our own impressions of things, true or false, but to the standard of convention. There are exceptions, but in general, if a man wants really penetrating judgments, really illuminating criticism on a classical author, he is ill advised if he goes to a classical scholar to get them. Again: You might perhaps expect that those whose chief occupation is the study of the greatest masters of style would insensibly acquire a good style of their own. It is not so: there are again exceptions, but as a rule the literary faculty of classical scholars is poor, and sometimes worse. A distinguished teacher of the classics, who now holds one of the most august positions in these realms, had occasion to give his reason for disapproving something or other, and he gave it in these words: 'It aggravates a tendency to let the thing slide.' We do not all of us write so ill as this, but we mostly write a style which is seldom graceful and not always grammatical: probably no class of students write English much worse. And as among the blind the one-eyed man is king, so the possessors of a very humble skill and grace in writing find themselves highly extolled if it is on classical themes that they write, because these merits are so unexpected, the standard is so low.

And while on the one hand no amount of classical learning can create a true appreciation of literature in those who lack the organs of appreciation, so on the other hand no great amount of classical learning is needed to quicken and refine the taste and judgment of those who do possess such organs. Who are the great critics of the classical literatures, the critics with real insight into the classical spirit, the critics who teach with authority and not as the scribes? They are such men as Lessing or Goethe or Matthew Arnold, scholars no doubt, but not scholars of minute or profound learning. Matthew Arnold went to his grave under the impression that the proper way to spell *lacrima* was to spell it with a *y*, and that the words ἀνδρὸς παιδοφόνοιο ποτὶ στόμα χεῖρ᾽ ὀρέγεσθαι meant 'to carry to my lips the hand of him that slew my son'. We pedants know better: we spell *lacrima* with an *i*, and we know that the verse of Homer really means 'to reach forth my hand to the chin of him that slew my son'. But when it comes to literary criticism, heap up in one scale all the literary criticism that the whole nation of professed scholars ever wrote, and drop into the other the thin green volume of Matthew Arnold's Lectures on Translating Homer, which has long been out of print because the British public does not care to read it, and the first scale, as Milton says, will straight fly up and kick the beam.

It appears then that upon the majority of mankind the classics can hardly be said to exert the transforming influence which is claimed for them. The special effect of a classical education on the majority of those who receive it, is not to transform and beautify their inner nature, but rather to confer a certain amount of polish on their surface, by teaching them things that one is expected to know and enabling them to understand the meaning of

English words and use them properly. If a man has learnt Greek and Latin and has to describe the blowing up of a powder mill, he will not describe it as a cataclysm; if he is irritated he will say so, and will not say that he is aggravated; if the conversation turns on the Muse who is supposed to preside over dancing, he will call her Terpsí-chŏre, and not Térpsitshoar. We shall probably therefore think it advisable to acquire a tincture of Classics, for ornament, just as we shall think it advisable to acquire a modicum of Science, for use. There, in both cases, we shall most of us stop; because to pursue the classics further in the expectation of transforming and beautifying our inner natures is, for most of us, to ask from those studies what they cannot give; and because, if practical utility be our aim in studying Science, a very modest amount of Science will serve our turn.

So we find that the two fancied aims of learning laid down by these two parties will not stand the test of examination. And no wonder; for these are the fabrications of men anxious to impose their own favourite pursuits on others, or of men who are ill at ease in their conscience until they have invented some external justification for those pursuits. The acquisition of knowledge needs no such justification: its true sanction is a much simpler affair, and inherent in itself. People are too prone to torment themselves with devising far-fetched reasons: they cannot be content with the simple truth asserted by Aristotle: 'all men possess by nature a craving for knowledge', πάντες ἄνθρωποι τοῦ εἰδέναι ὀρέγονται φύσει. This is no rare endowment scattered sparingly from heaven that falls on a few heads and passes others by: curiosity, the desire to know things as they are, is a craving no less native to the being of man, no less universal through mankind, than the craving for food and drink. And do you suppose that such a desire means nothing? The very definition of the good, says Aristotle again, is that which all desire. Whatever is pleasant is good, unless it can be shewn that in the long run it is harmful, or, in other words, not pleasant but unpleasant. Mr Spencer himself on another subject speaks thus: 'So profound an ignorance is there of the laws of life, that men do not even know that their sensations are their natural guides, and (when not rendered morbid by long continued disobedience) their trustworthy guides.' The desire of knowledge does not need, nor could it possibly possess, any higher or more authentic sanction than the happiness which attends its gratification.

Perhaps it will be objected that we see, every day of our lives, plenty of people who exhibit no pleasure in learning and experience no desire to know; people, as Plato agreeably puts it, who wallow in ignorance with the complacency of a brutal hog. We do; and here is the reason. If the cravings of hunger and thirst are denied satisfaction, if a man is kept from food and drink, the man starves to death, and there is an end of him. This is a result which arrests the attention of even the least observant mind; so it is generally recognised that hunger and thirst cannot be neglected with impunity, that a man ought to eat and drink. But if the craving for knowledge is denied satisfaction, the result which follows is not so striking to the eye. The man, worse luck, does not starve to death. He still preserves the aspect and motions of a living human being; so people think that the hunger and thirst for knowledge can be neglected with impunity. And yet, though the man does not die altogether, part of him dies, part of him starves to death: as Plato says, he never attains completeness and health, but walks lame to the end of his life and returns imperfect and good for nothing to the world below.

But the desire of knowledge, stifle it though you may, is

2   CH

none the less originally born with every man; and nature does not implant desires in us for nothing, nor endow us with faculties in vain. 'Sure,' says Hamlet,

> Sure, He that made us with such large discourse,
> Looking before and after, gave us not
> That capability and godlike reason
> To fust in us unused.

The faculty of learning is ours that we may find in its exercise that delight which arises from the unimpeded activity of any energy in the groove nature meant it to run in. Let a man acquire knowledge not for this or that external and incidental good which may chance to result from it, but for itself; not because it is useful or ornamental, but because it is knowledge, and therefore good for man to acquire. 'Brothers,' says Ulysses in Dante, when with his old and tardy companions he had left Seville on the right hand and Ceuta on the other, and was come to that narrow pass where Hercules assigned his landmarks to hinder man from venturing farther: 'Brothers, who through a hundred thousand dangers have reached the West, deny not, to this brief vigil of your senses that remains, experience of the unpeopled world behind the sunset. Consider of what seed ye are sprung: ye were not formed to live like brutes, but to follow virtue and knowledge.' For knowledge resembles virtue in this, and differs in this from other possessions, that it is not merely a means of procuring good, but is good in itself simply: it is not a coin which we pay down to purchase happiness, but has happiness indissolubly bound up with it. Fortitude and continence and honesty are not commended to us on the ground that they conduce, as on the whole they do conduce, to material success, nor yet on the ground that they will be rewarded hereafter: those whose office it is to exhort mankind to virtue are ashamed to degrade the cause they plead by proffering such lures as these. And let us too disdain to take lower ground in commending knowledge: let us insist that the pursuit of knowledge, like the pursuit of righteousness, is part of man's duty to himself; and remember the Scripture where it is written: 'He that refuseth instruction despiseth his own soul.'

I will not say, as Prof. Tyndall has somewhere said, that all happiness belongs to him who can say from his heart 'I covet truth'. Entire happiness is not attainable either by this or by any other method. Nay it may be urged on the contrary that the pursuit of truth in some directions is even injurious to happiness, because it compels us to take leave of delusions which were pleasant while they lasted. It may be urged that the light shed on the origin and destiny of man by the pursuit of truth in some directions is not altogether a cheerful light. It may be urged that man stands today in the position of one who has been reared from his cradle as the child of a noble race and the heir to great possessions, and who finds at his coming of age that he has been deceived alike as to his origin and his expectations; that he neither springs of the high lineage he fancied, nor will inherit the vast estate he looked for, but must put off his towering pride, and contract his boundless hopes, and begin the world anew from a lower level: and this, it may be urged, comes of pursuing knowledge. But even conceding this, I suppose the answer to be that knowledge, and especially disagreeable knowledge, cannot by any art be totally excluded even from those who do not seek it. Wisdom, said Aeschylus long ago, comes to men whether they will or no. The house of delusions is cheap to build, but draughty to live in, and ready at any instant to fall; and it is surely truer prudence to move our furniture betimes into the open air than to stay indoors until our tenement tumbles about our ears.   It is and it must in the long run be better for a man to see things as they are than to be ignorant of them; just as there is less fear of stumbling or of striking against corners in the daylight than in the dark.

Nor again will I pretend that, as Bacon asserts, 'the pleasure and delight of knowledge and learning far sur-passeth all other in nature'. This is too much the language of a salesman crying his own wares. The pleasures of the intellect are notoriously less vivid than either the pleasures of sense or the pleasures of the affections; and therefore, especially in the season of youth, the pursuit of knowledge is likely enough to be neglected and lightly esteemed in comparison with other pursuits offering much stronger immediate attractions. But the pleasure of learning and knowing, though not the keenest, is yet the least perishable of pleasures; the least subject to external things, and the play of chance, and the wear of time. And as a prudent man puts money by to serve as a provision for the material wants of his old age, so too he needs to lay up against the end of his days provision for the intellect. As the years go by, comparative values are found to alter: Time, says Sophocles, takes many things which once were pleasures and brings them nearer to pain. In the day when the strong men shall bow themselves, and desire shall fail, it will be a matter of yet more concern than now, whether one can say 'my mind to me a kingdom is'; and whether the windows of the soul look out upon a broad and delight-ful landscape, or face nothing but a brick wall.

Well then, once we have recognised that knowledge in itself is good for man, we shall need to invent no pretexts for studying this subject or that; we shall import no extra-neous considerations of use or ornament to justify us in learning one thing rather than another. If a certain depart-ment of knowledge specially attracts a man, let him study that, and study it because it attracts him; and let him not fabricate excuses for that which requires no excuse, but rest assured that the reason why it most attracts him is that it is best for him. The majority of mankind, as is only natural, will be most attracted by those sciences which most nearly concern human life; those sciences which, in Bacon's phrase, are drenched in flesh and blood, or, in the more elegant language of the *Daily Telegraph*, palpitate with actuality. The men who are attracted to the drier and the less palpitating sciences, say logic or pure mathematics or textual criticism, are likely to be fewer in number; but they are not to suppose that the comparative unpopularity of such learning renders it any the less worthy of pursuit. Nay they may if they like console themselves with Bacon's observation that 'this same *lumen siccum* doth parch and offend most men's watery and soft natures', and infer, if it pleases them, that their natures are less soft and watery than other men's. But be that as it may, we can all dwell together in unity without crying up our own pursuits or depreciating the pursuits of others on factitious grounds. We are not like the Ottoman sultans of old time, who thought they could never enjoy a moment's security till they had murdered all their brothers. There is no rivalry between the studies of Arts and Laws and Science but the rivalry of fellow-soldiers in striving which can most victoriously achieve the common end of all, to set back the frontier of darkness.

It is the glory of God, says Solomon, to conceal a thing: but the honour of kings is to search out a matter. Kings have long abdicated that province; and we students are come into their inheritance: it is our honour to search out the things which God has concealed. In Germany at Easter time they hide coloured eggs about the house and the garden that the children may amuse themselves in hunting after them and finding them. It is to some such game of hide-and-seek that we are invited by that power which planted in us the desire to find out what is concealed, and stored the universe with hidden things that we might delight ourselves in discovering them. And the pleasure of discovery differs from other pleasures in this, that it is shadowed by no fear of satiety on the one hand or of frustration on the other. Other desires perish in their gratification, but the desire of knowledge never: the eye is not satisfied with seeing nor the ear filled with hearing. Other desires become the occasion of pain through dearth of the material to gratify them, but not the desire of knowledge: the sum of things to be known is inexhaustible, and however long we read we shall never come to the end of our story-book. So long as the mind of man is what it is, it will continue to exult in advancing on the unknown throughout the infinite field of the universe; and the tree of knowledge will remain for ever, as it was in the beginning, a tree to be desired to make one wise.

II

FROM THE PREFACES

FOR a hundred years had men been editing Manilius and
had never advanced a step, when in 1579 there appeared at
Paris the first edition of Scaliger. This was reprinted at
Heidelberg in 1590 by Franciscus Iunius, who added
some insignificant notes of his own and a few conjectures
of more value by Matthaeus Lannoius, which Scaliger
stole as he pleased for his next edition: it is arrant gas-
conading when he says in the *Scaligerana* 'se et patrem
nihil umquam scripsisse, quod sciuissent ab aliis dictum
aut scriptum'. Not one good MS. had yet been brought
to light, and the transformation which first made Manilius
a legible author was the work of Scaliger's own unaided
wits; but for his second edition, issued at Leyden in 1600,
he obtained a collation of the Gemblacensis: the second
consequently excels the first almost as far as that excelled
all others. It is true that Scaliger in 1579 had often recovered by conjecture the true readings later found in G;
but the vulgate was in many parts too deeply falsified for
emendation, and nothing could help it but the knowledge
of a purer source. A third edition, corrected and enlarged
from Scaliger's manuscript notes, was published after his
death by I. H. Boeclerus at Strasburg in 1655, with addi-
tional remarks by T. Reinesius and I. Bullialdus.

Perhaps no critic has ever effected so great and permanent a change in any author's text as Scaliger in Manilius'.

Except the *Emendatio temporum*, which is too dissimilar
for comparison, this is his greatest work; and its virtues, if
they had fewer vices to keep them company, are such that
it is almost importunate to praise them. True, there is
luck as well as merit in the achievement: many of his
emendations required no Scaliger to make them, and were
made by Scaliger only because Manilius hitherto, instead
of finding a Beroaldus or Marullus to befriend him, had
fallen, as he was destined often to fall again, into the hands
of dullards. To write *tum di* for *tumidi* in 1 422 was a feat of
easy brilliancy, and such corrections are less of an honour
to Scaliger than a shame to his predecessors; but after all
deductions there remains enough to make a dozen editors
illustrious. The commentary is the one commentary on
Manilius, without forerunner and without successor; today, after the passage of three hundred years, it is the only
avenue to a study of the poem. He seems to have read
everything, Greek and Latin, published and unpublished,
which could explain or illustrate his author; and his vast
learning is carried lightly and imparted simply in terse
notes of moderate compass. Discursive he often is, and
sometimes vagrant, but even in digressions he neither
fatigues his readers like Casaubon nor bewilders them like
Salmasius. His style has not the ease and grace and Latinity
of Lambinus', but no commentary is brisker reading or
better entertainment than these abrupt and pithy notes,
with their spurts of mockery at unnamed detractors, and
their frequent and significant stress upon the difference
between Scaliger and a jackass.

There is a reverse to the medal, and I give it in the words
of his most intelligent enemy, Huet.

de poeta hoc praeclare meritum esse Scaligerum negari non potest;
nam et loca pleraque deplorata felicissime sanauit, multa etiam
obscura pro singulari sua eruditione illustrauit, nec pauca luxata,

perturbata, ac confusa pristinis sedibus solerter restituit. uerum dum nodum saepe quaerit in scirpo, nimia sua περιεργία, et anxia quadam ac morosa diligentia, tum et insano eruditionis ostentandae studio, egregium laborem corrupit. adeo ut quae Manilium legenti mihi clara saepe uisa fuerant et aperta, postquam Scaligeri notas consulueram, intricata eadem et obscura euaderent, neque ante rediret pristina lux, quam discussissem affusas ab eo tenebras, inductosque in planam et patentem uiam sentes purgassem.

In particular he will often propound interpretations which have no bearing either on his own text of Manilius or on any other, but pertain to things which he has read elsewhere, and which hang like mists in his memory and veil from his eyes the verses which he thinks he is explaining. Furthermore it must be said that Scaliger's conjectures in Manilius, as in all the other Latin poets whom he edited, are often uncouth and sometimes monstrous. 'Man darf,' says Haupt, *opusc.* III, p. 33, 'ohne Scaligers ruhm zu kränken, behaupten, dass kein grosser philolog neben sicheren entdeckungen des glänzendsten scharfsinnes so viel grammatisch unmögliches aufgestellt hat.' And the worse the conjecture the louder does Scaliger applaud himself. 'numquam felicius coniectura nobis cessit olim, quam in hoc inquinatissimo loco' says he at III 507. 'di meliora, uir magne,' replies Bentley, 'quam ut omnes tuae coniecturae ex hac censeantur. nam sensum aliquem in his inuestigo, nec ullum reperire queo.'

Barth's *Aduersaria* published in 1624 devote a good deal of space to Manilius without much result. To read 3000 tall columns of close print by a third-rate scholar is no proper occupation for mortals; but by means of the index I have unearthed his Manilian conjectures, futile for the most part but now and again of surprising merit: the best of them are usually ignored or attributed to later critics. * * * Salmasius, in those inimitable monuments of erudition and untidiness his *Diatribae de annis climactericis* and his

Plinianae Exercitationes, busied though he is with astrology and astronomy, does very little for the criticism or interpretation of Manilius. Manilius' best friend in that generation, and the greatest critic, after Bentley and Scaliger, whose attention he ever engaged, was Gronouius, who in his four famous books of *Obseruationes* has filled many pages and chapters with admirable corrections of the *Astronomica*.

In 1675 Sir Edward Sherburne published a translation of the first book into English verse, with ample notes displaying a wide reading but no great acuteness or alertness of mind. Another metrical version of the whole poem was produced by Thomas Creech in 1700. In 1697 appeared the Delphin edition by Michael Fayus or du Fay, a slovenly work, but yet deserving less neglect than it receives. The commentary, though neither learned nor accurate, contains a good deal of miscellaneous information and has its humble use; the paraphrase explains correctly many things which Scaliger had misinterpreted; the text, which seems to have composed itself without the help or knowledge of the editor, combines a mass of blunders and a sprinkling of Scaliger's readings with a certain number of corrections which I have found in no earlier book and have therefore assigned to Fayus. But the edition owes its worth to an appendix of 88 pages contributed by Pierre Daniel Huet sometime bishop of Avranches, 'animaduersiones in Manilium et Scaligeri notas,' which perhaps deserves to be reckoned as the chief piece of work on Manilius in the age between Scaliger and Bentley. It includes a considerable sum of emendations, less brilliant and important than Gronouius' but yet skilful and judicious, a long series of admirably clear and accurate and erudite interpretations, and a running fire of polemical comment upon Scaliger, often wrong but much oftener right. Huet was a critic of uncommon exactness, sobriety, and malevolence, whose naturally keen wits were sharpened to a finer edge by his dislike of Scaliger. He frankly owns in chapter v of the Huetiana 'je n'ai écrit sur Manile que pour faire voir que dans les trois éditions de ce Poëte il [Scaliger] a entassé fautes sur fautes et ignorances sur ignorances'. Hence it happens, in the irony of human affairs, that he, the shrewd and accomplished Huet, is now excessively admired by the dull, who cherish a timid enmity for great and victorious innovators, and delight to see them rapped over the knuckles by Huet or anyone else who has the requisite address. His services to Manilius are not so many and great as to estrange the affection of these admirers; indeed it would be hard to find 300 verses in a row for which Scaliger has not done more than Huet did for all five books together. Perhaps if he had been less bent on harming Scaliger he might have helped Manilius more: at any rate it is matter for some surprise and dis-appointment that so competent a critic should after all have done so little where there was so much to do. But the fact is that his mind had keenness without force, and was not a trenchant instrument. His corrections, deft as they are, touch only the surface of the text; his precise and lucid explanations are seldom explanations of difficulties, but only dispel perverse misunderstandings of things which hardly any one but Scaliger can ever have misunderstood. When a real obscurity had baffled Scaliger, it baffled Huet, and was reprieved till the advent of Bentley.

Lucida tela diei: these are the words that come into one's mind when one has halted at some stubborn perplexity of reading or interpretation, has witnessed Scaliger and Gronouius and Huetius fumble at it one after another, and then turns to Bentley and sees Bentley strike his finger on the place and say *thou ailest here, and here.* His Manilius is a greater work than either the Horace or the Phalaris; yet its subject condemns it to find few readers, and those few for the most part unfit: to be read by Dorville and left unread by Madvig. Haupt alone† has praised it in proportion to its merit. * * * Had Bentley never edited Manilius, Nicolaus Heinsius would be the foremost critic of Latin poetry; but this is a work beyond the scope of even Heinsius. Great as was Scaliger's achievement it is yet surpassed and far surpassed by Bentley's: Scaliger at the side of Bentley is no more than a marvellous boy. In mere quantity indeed the corrections of the critic who came first may be the more imposing, but it is significant that Scaliger accomplished most in the easiest parts of the poem and Bentley in the hardest. The firm strength and piercing edge and arrowy swiftness of his intellect, his matchless facility and adroitness and resource, were never so triumphant as where defeat seemed sure; and yet it is other virtues that one most admires and welcomes as one turns from the smoky fire of Scaliger's genius to the sky and air of Bentley's: his lucidity, his sanity, his just and simple and straightforward fashion of thought. His emendations are only a part, though the most conspicuous part, of his services to Manilius; for here, as in Horace, there are many passages which he was the first to vindicate from mistaken conjecture by discovering their true interpretation. He had furnished himself too with fresh and efficacious tools: he had procured not only the use of G but collations of L and also, more important, of V, which first

† All that F. A. Wolf can find to say of it is this, *litt. anal.* 1, pp. 61 *sq.*: 'ein Drittheil Änderungen weniger würde der mit Conjecturen überfüllten Ausgabe mehr genützt, und dem Kritiker viele gegründete Vorwürfe erspart haben.' Wolf, like all pretenders to encyclopedic knowledge, had a dash of the impostor about him, and we have no assurance that he had read the book which he thus presumes to judge. Even if he had really read it he was little qualified to estimate its value. What he says of it is not false: the falsehood lies in what he does not say.

revealed in a clear form the tradition of the second family; and from II 665 or 668, where V begins, to the end of the poem, his incomparable skill and judgment in the use of MSS. have left but little in this department for his successors to do, provided they have the wit, or in default of that the modesty, to follow his example.

The faults of this edition, which are abundant, are the faults of Bentley's other critical works. He was impatient, he was tyrannical, and he was too sure of himself. Hence he corrupts sound verses which he will not wait to understand, alters what offends his taste without staying to ask about the taste of Manilius, plies his desperate hook upon corruptions which do not yield at once to gentler measures, and treats the MSS. much as if they were fellows of Trinity. Nay more: though Bentley's faculty for discovering truth has no equal in the history of learning, his wish to discover it was not so strong. Critics like Porson and Lachmann, inferior in εὐστοχία and ἀγχίνοια, put him to shame by their serious and disinterested purpose and the honesty of their dealings with themselves. His buoyant mind, elated by the exercise of its powers, too often forgot the nature of its business, and turned from work to play; and many a time when he feigned and half fancied that he was correcting the scribe, he knew in his heart (and of his *Paradise Lost* they tell us he confessed it) that he was revising the author.

It is a point in which Bentley compares ill with Scaliger, that his conjectures often leave the MSS. too far behind them and sometimes set them utterly at naught. The crowning instance is v 229 *aut cornua tauri* for *atque arma ferarum*. But the worst that can be said of this conjecture is that it is improbable to the last degree: dozens and scores of Scaliger's, distant only a letter or two from the MSS., are something very much worse; they are impossible. Bentley's rashness there is no denying, but it is less than Scaliger's. Again: he will now and then propose conjectures which instead of amending the text make havoc of it; and II 322 *nongentae*, III 421 *lucis*, 547 *mensibus*, are very amazing blunders. But they amaze because they are Bentley's: in Scaliger such things occur on every second page, and the reader ceases to wonder at them.

It was one of Bentley's chief services to the text that he first detected the presence there of spurious verses. But this discovery, like Scaliger's discovery of transpositions in Propertius, was misused and perverted by its own author till its utility was well-nigh cancelled and its credit annulled. When a genuine verse was so corrupt that no meaning glimmered through it, and even Bentley's divination was baffled at the first assault, then the impatient critic, who had no turn for tiresome blockades, chastised its recalcitrancy by proclaiming it counterfeit. He forgot that counterfeit verses are not wont to be meaningless unless they are corrupt as well, and that the aim of interpolators is not to make difficulties but to remove them. The best prize that Bentley missed, and the richest province left for his successors, is the correction of those verses of Manilius which he precipitately and despotically expelled.

To edit Manilius was one of Bentley's earliest projects, and he writes on p. lxiii of the preface to Phalaris 'I had prepared a Manilius for the press, which had been published already (1699), had not the dearness of paper and the want of good types, and some other occasions, hindered'. The edition was brought out in 1739, when Bentley was seventy-seven, by his nephew and namesake; and such notes as that on v 404 declare that it was even yet unfinished. One other student of Manilius in this period deserves a word, the brilliant and erratic Withof, whose manuscript conjectures, often identical with Bentley's, are preserved in the library of Goettingen and mentioned by Jacob.

If a man will comprehend the richness and variety of the universe, and inspire his mind with a due measure of wonder and of awe, he must contemplate the human intellect not only on its heights of genius but in its abysses of ineptitude; and it might be fruitlessly debated to the end of time whether Richard Bentley or Elias Stoeber was the more marvellous work of the Creator: Elias Stoeber, whose reprint of Bentley's text, with a commentary intended to confute it, saw the light in 1767 at Strasburg, a city still famous for its geese. This commentary is a performance in comparison with which the *Aetna* of Mr S. Sudhaus is a work of science and of genius. Stoeber's mind, though that is no name to call it by, was one which turned as unswervingly to the false, the meaningless, the unmetrical, and the ungrammatical, as the needle to the pole. His purpose, put in short, is to depose good MSS., G and L and V, in favour of a bad MS., 'Parisinus uere Regius', and to depose great critics, Scaliger and especially Bentley, in favour of Regiomontanus, who was no critic at all.

Pour expliquer les leçons ridicules de ces deux oracles [says Pingré with perfect justice], et leur donner quelque vernis de sens commun, on accumule des solécismes, des barbarismes, des verbes sans nominatifs, des nominatifs et des accusatifs sans verbes, des subjonctifs et infinitifs que rien ne gouverne, des constructions inintelligibles, des mots expliqués dans un sens qui ne fut jamais le leur, défauts de suite, défauts de sens, contradictions, sous-ententes inadmissibles, fautes grossières de quantité, termes parfaitement inutiles, qu'en langage de collège on appelle *chevilles*. Voilà tout ce que nous avons pu recueillir des notes de Maître Elie Stoeber; et M. Elie Stoeber trouve cela très-élégant, très-digne de l'esprit sublime et délicat de Manilius.

A bare mention is enough for Edmund Burton's edition of 1783, with a text founded on the first recension of Scaliger, an assortment of borrowed notes, and a few invectives against Bentley. No more does it concern us that the Societas Bipontina issued a text of Manilius with their Virgil of the same year. This edition contains a 'notitia literaria de M. Manilio', whose history is divided, after the fashion of Hesiod, into 'aetas I, autographa et genuina, 1472–1566. aetas II, ambigua seu Scaligerana, 1579–1739. aetas III, deformata ab aggressione Richardi Bentleji, Angli.'

In the same year 1783 died Iohannes Schrader, Heinsius dimidiatus, whose conjectures on Manilius are preserved in manuscript among Santen's books (no. 95) at Berlin and are mentioned by Jacob pp. xiii sq. The youth of Berlin and Goettingen might easily be worse employed than in transcribing the notes of Schrader and Withof and giving them to the world after the pattern of Mr E. Hedicke's *Studia Bentleiana*. I suspect that they have forestalled a good many of my own conjectures; but I have abstained from all enquiry after them, in order that the coincidence, if coincidence there be, may weigh the heavier.

In 1786 appeared at Paris in two volumes the text of A. G. Pingré, with a French translation or rather paraphrase facing it, and a frugal equipment of brief notes textual and explanatory. Pingré, though intelligent and well-read, was no marvel of learning or brilliancy or penetration; but the prime virtue of a critic, worth all the rest, he had: simplicity and rectitude of judgment. The text is Bentley's, improved by the subtraction of many unnecessary or extravagant conjectures; and though it not only retains much of Bentley which ought to be omitted but omits much which ought to be retained, it is yet even now, in the year 1903, the best and far the best existing text of Manilius. Pingré's own conjectures are not many, but sensible and sometimes excellent; and the translation, though it grows reprehensibly vague and wordy where the text has no meaning or where its meaning is obscure to Pingré, is the student's smoothest way to a continuous understanding of the poem. In no edition of Manilius is there so little that calls for censure.

There is nothing to speak of between Pingré and Friedrich Jacob, who in the years 1832–6 put forth at Lubeck a series of five pamphlets successfully defending a number of the verses condemned by Bentley, and produced in 1846 what remained for the rest of the century the commonly accepted text. Bentley is first, and Scaliger second, among the conjectural emendators of Manilius, and there is no third; but if there were a third it would be Jacob. Say what you will, he has contributed to the *Astronomica*, as to the *Aetna* twenty years before, a body of corrections not only considerable in number but often of the most arresting ingenuity and penetration. Yet the virtues of his work are quenched and smothered by the multitude and monstrosity of its vices. They say that he was born of human parentage; but if so he must have been suckled by Caucasian tigers. * * * Not only had Jacob no sense for grammar, no sense for coherency, no sense for sense, but being himself possessed by a passion for the clumsy and the hispid he imputed this disgusting taste to all the authors whom he edited; and Manilius, the one Latin poet who excels even Ovid in verbal point and smartness, is accordingly constrained to write the sort of poetry which might have been composed by Nebuchadnezzar when he was driven from men and did eat grass as oxen.

> tene feris dignam tantum, Germania, matrem
> dixerat iniusti musa mathematici?
> at sua nunc illi criticus te matre creatus
> effecit tantum carmina digna fera.

In his dealing with the MSS. this blunderer has learnt no lesson from the chief master of the art, but conceives a spite against G and makes a pet of the Vossianus secundus (that is not only V but v, a poor kinsman of G's family); and this codex, from which the skill and tact of Bentley had drawn more profit to Manilius than from any other, becomes in Jacob's hands an engine of depravation. In the notes with which he now and again supports his corruptions and misinterpretations of the text he seems to stick at no falsehood and no absurdity which the pen will consent to trace on paper. In short his book, if only its vices are considered, is a scarce less woful piece of work than Stoeber's: the difference is that, while Stoeber never reminds one of a rational animal, the fog of Jacob's intellect is shot through, and that not seldom, by flashes of conspicuous and startling brilliancy. They are Capricorn and Sagittarius: *pars huic hominis, sed nulla priori*.

*　　*　　*　　*　　*　　*

Some ancient authors have descended to modern times in one MS. only, or in a few MSS. derived immediately or with little interval from one. Such are Lucretius, Catullus, Valerius Flaccus, and Statius in his *Siluae*. Others there are whose text, though in the main reposing on a single copy, can be corrected here and there from others, inferior indeed, but still independent and indispensable. Such are Juvenal, Ovid in his *Heroides*, Seneca in his tragedies, and Statius in his *Thebais* and *Achilleis*. There is a third class whose text comes down from a remote original through separate channels, and is preserved by MSS. of unlike character but like fidelity, each serving in its turn to correct the faults of others. Such are Persius, Lucan, Martial, and Manilius.

If I had no judgment, and knew it, and were nevertheless immutably resolved to edit a classic, I would single out my victim from the first of these three classes: that would be best for the victim and best for me. Authors surviving in a solitary MS. are by far the easiest to edit, because their editor is relieved from one of the most exacting offices of criticism, from the balancing of evidence and the choice of variants. They are the easiest, and for a fool they are the safest. One field at least for the display of folly is denied him: others are open, and in defending, correcting, and explaining the written text he may yet aspire to make a scarecrow of the author and a byword of himself; but with no variants to afford him scope for choice and judgment he cannot exhibit his impotence to judge and choose.

But the worst of having no judgment is that one never misses it, and buoyantly embarks without it upon enterprises in which it is not so much a convenience as a necessity. Hence incompetent editors are not found flocking to texts like Valerius Flaccus' and leaving texts like Manilius' alone. They essay to edit the latter no less promptly than the former; and then comes the pinch. They find themselves unexpectedly committed to a business which demands not only the possession, but the constant exercise, of intellectual faculties. An editor of no judgment, perpetually confronted with a couple of MSS. to choose from, cannot but feel in every fibre of his being that he is a donkey between two bundles of hay. What shall he do now? Leave criticism to critics, you may say, and betake himself to any honest trade for which he is less unfit. But he prefers a more flattering solution: he confusedly imagines that if one bundle of hay is removed he will cease to be a donkey.

So he removes it. Are the two MSS. equal, and do they bewilder him with their rival merit and exact from him at every other moment the novel and distressing effort of using his brains? Then he pretends that they are not equal: he calls one of them 'the best MS.,' and to this he resigns the editorial functions which he is himself unable to discharge. He adopts its readings when they are better than its fellow's, adopts them when they are no better, adopts them when they are worse: only when they are impossible, or rather when he perceives their impossibility, is he dislodged from his refuge and driven by stress of weather to the other port.

This method answers the purpose for which it was devised: it saves lazy editors from working and stupid editors from thinking. But somebody has to pay for these luxuries, and that somebody is the author; since it must follow, as the night the day, that this method should falsify his text. Suppose, if you will, that the editor's 'best MS.' is in truth the best: his way of using it is none the less ridiculous. To believe that wherever a best MS. gives possible readings it gives true readings, and that only where it gives impossible readings does it give false readings, is to believe that an incompetent editor is the darling of Providence, which has given its angels charge over him lest at any time his sloth and folly should produce their natural results and incur their appropriate penalty. Chance and the common course of nature will not bring it to pass that the readings of a MS. are right wherever they are possible and impossible wherever they are wrong: that needs divine intervention; and when one considers the history of man and the spectacle of the universe I hope one may say without impiety that divine intervention might have been better employed elsewhere. How the world is managed, and why it was created, I cannot tell; but it is no feather-bed for the repose of sluggards.

Apart from its damage to the author, it might perhaps be thought that this way of editing would bring open scorn upon the editors, and that the whole reading public would rise up and tax them, as I tax them now, with ignorance of their trade and dereliction of their duty. But the public is soon disarmed. This planet is largely inhabited by parrots, and it is easy to disguise folly by giving it a fine name. Those who live and move and have their being in the world of words and not of things, and employ language less as a vehicle than as a substitute for thought, are readily duped by the assertion that this stolid adherence to a favourite MS., instead of being, as it is, a private and personal necessity imposed on certain editors by their congenital defects, is a principle; and that its name is 'scientific criticism' or 'critical method'. This imposture is helped by the fact that there really are such things as scientific methods and principles of criticism, and that the 19th century was specially distinguished by a special application of these methods and principles which is easily confused, by parrots, with the unprincipled and unmethodical practice now in question. Till 1800 and later no attempt was made by scholars to determine the genealogy and affiliation of MSS.: science and method, applied to this end by the generation of Bekker and Lachmann, Madvig and Cobet, have cast hundreds of MSS., once deemed authorities, on the dust-heap, have narrowed the circle of witnesses by excluding those who merely repeat what they have heard from others, and have proved that the text of certain authors reposes on a single document from which all other extant MSS. are copied. Hence it is no hard task to diffuse among parrots the notion that an editor who assigns preponderant authority to any single MS. is following the principles of critical science, since the question whether the MS. really possesses that authority is one which does not suggest itself to the creature of which Pliny has written 'capiti eius duritia eadem quae rostro'. Nay more: the public is predisposed in favour of the falsehood, and has reasons for wishing to believe it true. Tell the average man that inert adhesion to one authority is methodical criticism, and you tell him good news: I too, thinks he, have the makings of a methodical critic about me. 'Man kann nur etwas aussprechen,' said Goethe, 'was dem Eigendünkel und der Bequemlichkeit schmeichelt, um eines grossen Anhanges in der mittelmässigen Menge gewiss zu sein.'

But still there is a hitch. Competent editors exist; and side by side with those who have embraced 'the principles of criticism', there are those who follow the practice of critics: who possess intellects, and employ them on their work. Consequently their work is better done, and the contrast is mortifying. This is not as it should be. As the wise man dieth, so dieth the fool: why then should we allow them to edit the classics differently? If nature, with flagitious partiality, has given judgment and industry to some men and left other men without them, it is our evident duty to amend her blind caprice; and those who are able and willing to think must be deprived of their unfair advantage by stringent prohibitions. In Association football you must not use your hands, and similarly in textual criticism you must not use your brains. Since we cannot make fools behave like wise men, we will insist that wise men should behave like fools: by these means only can we redress the injustice of nature and anticipate the equality of the grave.

To this end, not only has the simple process of opening one's mouth and shutting one's eyes been dignified by the title of 'eine streng wissenschaftliche Methode', but rational criticism has been branded with a term of formal reprobation. 'Butter and honey shall he eat,' says Isaiah of Immanuel, '*that he may know to refuse the evil and choose the good*.' This is a very bad system of education: to refuse the evil and choose the good is 'der reinste Eclecticismus'.

By this use of tickets it is rendered possible, in a world where names are mistaken for things, not only to be thoughtless and

idle without discredit, but even to be vain of your vices and
to reprove your neighbour for his lack of them. It is rendered
possible to pamper self-complacency while indulging lazi-
ness; and the 'scientific critic', unlike the rest of mankind,
contrives to enjoy in combination the usually incompatible
luxuries of shirking his work and despising his superiors.

*   *   *   *   *   *

But no more dismal example of an author corrupted
through and through by the very means which fortune
has ordained for his preservation and restitution is anywhere to be found than the two last editions of Manilius.
To elude what Byron calls 'the blight of life—the demon
Thought,' Messrs Jacob and Bechert have committed
themselves respectively to the Vossianus and the Gemblacensis, the devil and the deep sea. Having small literary
culture they are not revolted by illiteracy, having slight
knowledge of grammar they are not revolted by solecism,
having no sequence of ideas they are not revolted by in-
coherency, having nebulous thoughts they are not revolted
by nonsense: on the contrary the illiterate and ungrammatical and inconsecutive and meaningless things with
which both MSS. abound are supposed by their respective
votaries to be 'Manilian', and each believes himself a
connoisseur of the poet's peculiar style. Strange to say,
their conception of that style is identical; and the two texts,
though based on opposite authorities and diverging in
innumerable details, have in their general aspect a conspicuous and frightful similarity. The Manilian peculiarities
of V are just like the Manilian peculiarities of G, for the
simple reason that they are neither Manilian nor peculiar.
They are ordinary corruptions; and Jacob can see that this
is so in G, and Bechert can see it in V. And after all,

though they may mount their hobbies, they cannot stick in the saddle. Again and again their favourites offer readings which they are forced to abandon, and to accept the readings of the rival MSS.; but these lessons they hasten to forget, and are no wiser next time.

Thus far of the places where our MSS. dissent, and the reading of their archetype is to be regained by choice and comparison. Where they agree, there the text of the archetype is before us, an archetype, like themselves, corrupt and interpolated; and now begins the business of correcting this. But first, in every place where the tradition is thus clearly ascertained, comes the question whether this be not itself the truth; and it is no simple question. The Romans are foreigners and write to please themselves, not us; Latin poets compose Latin poetry, which is very unlike English or German poetry; and each writer has his own peculiarities and the peculiarities of his generation and his school, which must be learnt by observation and cannot be divined by taste. In Manilius, an author both corrupt and difficult, who since the revival of learning has had few competent students, it is no cause for wonder that even after Scaliger and Bentley there remains as much to explain as to emend, and that these toiling giants, amidst loads of rubbish, have carted away some fragments of the fabric. A properly informed and properly attentive reader will find that many verses hastily altered by some editors and absurdly defended by others can be made to yield a just sense without either changing the text or inventing a new Latinity; and I think that I have often vindicated the MSS. by a reasonable explanation in passages where my betters had assailed them.

But those who can understand what Scaliger and Bentley and Gronouius and Heinsius and Lachmann could not understand are now so numerous, and their daily exploits in hermeneutics are so repulsive and deterrent, that I have avoided nothing so anxiously as this particular mode of being ridiculous; and it is likely enough that my dread of seeming to march with the times has led me here and there to err on the side of caution, and timidly to alter what I might without rashness have defended. * * *

The art of explaining corrupt passages instead of correcting them is imagined by those who now practise it to be something new, a discovery of these last twenty years. But man is not thus tardy in devising follies. Wakefield's Lucretius, to go no further back, is a stately monument of the craft; Goerenz plied it busily in Cicero and Fickert in Seneca before ever Mr Buecheler wrote a word, and in Alschefski's Livy the style produced a masterpiece as yet unrivalled by Mr Sudhaus himself. What stamps the last twenty years with their special character is not the presence of such scholars as these but the absence of great scholars. During the other part of the 19th century, before the North-German school had entered on its decline, critics of this order were no less plentiful than now,—*the poor shall never cease out of the land* says the scripture,—but they were cowed and kept under by critics of another order. Today this tyranny is overpast: the Lachmanns and Madvigs are gone, the Mosers and Forbigers remain; and now they lift up their heads and rejoice aloud at the emancipation of human incapacity. History repeats itself, and we now witness in Germany pretty much what happened in England after 1825, when our own great age of scholarship, begun in 1691 by Bentley's *Epistola ad Millium*, was ended by the successive strokes of doom which consigned Dobree and Elmsley to the grave and Blomfield to the bishopric of Chester. England disappeared from the fellowship of nations for the next forty years: Badham, the one English scholar of the mid-century whose reputation crossed the Channel, received from abroad the praises of Duebner and Nauck and Cobet, but at home was excluded from academical preferment, set to teach boys at Birmingham, and finally transported to the antipodes: his countrymen, having turned their backs on Europe and science and the past, sat down to banquet on mutual approbation, to produce the Classical Museum and the Bibliotheca Classica, and to perish without a name. I will not be unjust, and I hasten to add that no modern German editor with whom I am acquainted is quite so ignorant as the average English editor of those days: the resemblance lies in the determination to explain what the MSS. happen to offer, and the self-complacency which this frame of mind begets. It does not seem to strike these gentlemen that if their practice is right the practice of those great men who in the last century won for Germany the captaincy of European scholarship was wrong; that this recurrence to the methods of Wakefield must acknowledge itself to be what it is, a revolt from the methods of Lachmann; and that living Germans cannot long continue to trade upon the reputation of dead Germans whose principles they have abandoned and reversed. They now pretend that the relapse of the last twenty years is not a reaction against the great work of their elders, but a supplement to it. To the Lachmanns and Bentleys and Scaligers they politely ascribe the quality of *Genialität*: there is a complementary virtue called *Umsicht*, and this they ascribe to themselves. Why, I cannot tell: apparently by a process of reasoning which may be thrown into the following syllogism:

> turpe ac miserum est nec cautum esse nec ingeniosum et
>   tamen poetas Latinos edere uelle;
> ego autem ingeniosus non sum:
> sum ergo cautus.

For assuredly there is no trade on earth, excepting textual criticism, in which the name of prudence would be given to that habit of mind which in ordinary human life is called credulity.

The average man, if he meddles with criticism at all, is a conservative critic. His opinions are determined not by his reason, —'the bulk of mankind' says Swift 'is as well qualified for flying as for thinking,'—but by his passions; and the faintest of all human passions is the love of truth. He believes that the text of ancient authors is generally sound, not because he has acquainted himself with the elements of the problem, but because he would feel uncomfortable if he did not believe it; just as he believes, on the same cogent evidence, that he is a fine fellow, and that he will rise again from the dead. And since the classical public, like all other publics, is chiefly composed of average men, he is encouraged to hold this belief and to express it. But beside this general cause there are peculiar circumstances which explain and even excuse the present return to superstition. At the end of the great age, in the sixties and seventies, conjecture was employed, and that by very eminent men, irrationally. Ritschl's dealings with Plautus and Nauck's with the Attic tragedians were violent and arbitrary beyond all bounds: and their methods were transferred to the sphere of dactylic poetry by Baehrens, a man of vast energy and vigorous intelligence but of unripe judgment and faulty scholarship, who with one hand conferred on the Latin poets more benefits than any critic since Lachmann and with the other imported ten times as many corruptions as he removed.

This could not last, and a student of the world's history might have predicted what has now ensued. Error, if allowed to run its course, secures its own downfall, and is sooner or later overthrown, not by the truth, but by error of an opposite kind. When this misuse of conjecture had disgusted not only the judicious but the greater number of the injudicious, there followed a recoil, and it now became the fashion, instead of correcting the handiwork of poets, to interpret the handiwork of scribes. The conservative reaction was chiefly fostered by the teaching and example of Messrs Vahlen and Buecheler: men of wide learning and no mean acuteness, but without simplicity of judgment. Once set going by critics of repute, the movement, commended by its very nature to the general public, has prospered as downhill movements do; and its original leaders, as usually happens to those who instruct mankind in easy and agreeable vices, are far outdone by their disciples. In racing back to the feet of Alschefski Messrs Buecheler and Vahlen are hampered by two grave encumbrances: they know too much Latin, and they are not sufficiently obtuse. Among their pupils are several who comprehend neither Latin nor any other language, and whom nature has prodigally endowed at birth with that hebetude of intellect which Messrs Vahlen and Buecheler, despite their assiduous and protracted efforts, have not yet succeeded in acquiring. Thus equipped, the apprentices proceed to exegetical achievements of which their masters are incapable, and which perhaps inspire those masters less with envy than with fright: indeed I imagine that Mr Buecheler, when he first perused Mr Sudhaus' edition of the *Aetna*, must have felt something like Sin when she gave birth to Death.

2. MANILIUS V (1930)[2]

From the MSS. I now proceed to the efflorescence of editions which has enriched the opening of the 20th century.

In 1907, his 83rd year, Breiter published the first volume, text with apparatus criticus, of the edition which he had been meditating for a lifetime; the second, a commentary, followed in 1908, a few months before his death. Though slender in bulk and unpretentious in character they were hailed by his countrymen as a 'gigantisches Lebenswerk' and a 'monumentum aere perennius deutschen Gelehrten-fleisses'; 'Durch ihren hohen wissenschaftlichen Wert tritt Br.'s Ausgabe den Arbeiten Scaligers, Bentleys und'— eloquent conjunction—'Pingrés würdig zur Seite'; 'Die Wissenschaft ist um ein monumentales Hilfsmittel für das Verständnis dieses schweren Dichters bereichert, der Studierende hat einen zuverlässigen Führer gewonnen: immensus labor est et fertilis idem!' This ought not to be forgotten, and the reader should bear it steadily in mind as he peruses what I am about to say.

Breiter's papers in Fleckeisen's *Neue Jahrbuecher*, vol. 139 (1889) and vol. 147 (1893), were the most estimable contribution made to the study of Manilius after Jacob's edition. The corrections of Ellis were rather more numerous, and one or two of them were very pretty, but his readers were in perpetual contact with the intellect of an idiot child: in Breiter's articles the good preponderated, and he thought and wrote like a sane man and a grown man. His edition therefore, when at last it came, was a severe disappointment; and on a general view it detracts from his merit. It was not senile, but it showed that an edition was an undertaking beyond his powers.

His recension is to be commended in so far as it maintains a fairly just balance between the rival MSS. and avoids the bias of Bechert on one side and of Jacob on the other; but his use and choice of emendation was haphazard, and his own new conjectures, extorted by the task of editing, were without exception worthless. In his apparatus criticus he

persisted in retaining the cod. Cusanus, because he was
much too old to take example by me; he wantonly deceived
the less wary of his readers with an inaccurate collation of
G, which others had collated accurately; and his collation
of L, which should have been a boon and a blessing,
because much fuller and more minute than Bechert's, was
an insidious peril and a pernicious nuisance. His eyesight
was evidently feeble, and did not serve him well in collat-
ing MSS. or correcting proofs; but that is not enough to
account for the bucketfuls of falsehood which he discharged
on an ignorant and confiding public. In book III, which
is much the shortest book, his apparatus, consisting of
fewer than 350 lines, contains more than 110 definitely
false statements: I do not reckon its frequent and deceitful
omissions, nor the equally deceitful consequences of the
editor's ignorance of his trade. * * *

The commentary is plain and concise, but meagre, and
a student without other resource would starve on it. It
makes no pretence whatever to 'wissenschaftlichen Wert'.
Breiter's chief purpose was to explain for novices the
astrology of the poem, but his knowledge of the subject
was neither original nor adequate. Verbal interpretation
is often lacking, critical discussion is generally shunned,
and Latinity gets little attention. Falsehoods, blunders of
every sort and size, self-contradictions, misinterpretations,
miscalculations, misquotations and misprints leave few
pages undisfigured.

In 1911 an elaborate edition of the Second book was
produced by Mr H. W. Garrod. I declined to review it
on its publication, leaving it a fair field in which it received
no competent criticism except from Mr J. G. Smyly in
Hermathena 1912, pp. 137–68. Mr Garrod brought to his
task activity and energy, a brisk intelligence, and a strong
desire to shine. His book, unlike the work of a later editor,

was the fruit of independent investigation, diversified reading and genuine industry. The most valuable part of its
contents was the new and enlarged knowledge of the cod.
Venetus provided by his discovery of Gronouius' collation
in the margin of a book of Bentley's. There is one passage,
681 sq., which Mr Garrod, though not the first to understand it, was the first to explain, because the interpreters
had not understood it; but I do not think that any other of
his interpretations is both new and true. His conjectures
were singularly cheap and shallow, and his impatience of
more circumspect emendators, such as Bentley, broke out
at 689 in insolence. The apparatus criticus is neither skilful
nor careful, often defective and sometimes visibly so; I
have counted more than 60 positive misstatements, of which
only a minority can be laid at Breiter's door. The translation is dexterous and serviceable, but has an average of
more than three false renderings to the page, not counting
the suppression of inconvenient words and the insertion
of convenient ones. Some of his interpretations were so
little pondered that he changed them in the course of his
work without perceiving it: there are more than a dozen
places where translation and commentary contradict one
another, and at 409 discrepancy is not confined to them.
An astrological figure on p. 146, borrowed from others, is
false in four particulars to the editor's own text. The
commentary, which is full and mainly original, contains
much more truth than error, but it contains so much error
that the only readers who can use it with safety are those
whose knowledge extends beyond Mr Garrod's; though
even a student quite ignorant of the subject must discover,
if intelligent and attentive, that some things which the
editor tells him, for instance at 361–70, cannot possibly be
true. * * * But this seems to be a sort of English book
which Germans admire, as they once admired Wakefield's

Lucretius, and it was greeted as 'Garrods trefflicher Kommentar', 'das herrliche Werk', 'das vortreffliche Buch'. There were no such bouquets for me; and perhaps the reader will do well to consider how far my judgment of Mr Garrod's performance may have been warped by the passion of envy.

It is comprehensible that Breiter and Mr Garrod should aspire to edit Manilius, or a book of Manilius, and should attempt the enterprise; but why Jakob van Wageningen took it into his head that the world would be the better for an edition from him, and fetched his paste and scissors to this particular spot, I cannot imagine.

For the text which he published with Teubner in 1915 he professed to have collated G and L himself and to have procured photographs of M. Yet the apparatus criticus contains more than 200 false reports of the MSS., and much of this falsehood is borrowed falsehood. In book III alone there are 25 places where he has copied Breiter's mistakes instead of consulting the MSS. themselves; and some of those mistakes are gross indeed. * * * The number of conjectures which he ascribes to those who were not their authors is nearer 300 than 200; and although my editions of books I and II had already appeared, and correction was there if he wanted it, he would not look. He had not learnt to write an apparatus criticus. * * * He had not even learnt to read an apparatus criticus; he shows ignorance of the lections of the cod. Flor. in dozens of places where Bechert's silence had made them known to every instructed student. The text is neither conservative nor intelligently amended; conjectures are admitted without respect of merit, the last dregs of Breiter and the topmost froth of Mr Garrod are gulped down together, and the MSS. are nowhere more readily deserted than where their tradition is sound. Of his own conjectures, which are few, I can accept only one. The index is almost as full of errors as the apparatus criticus. * * *

The Latin commentary was separately published in 1921 with no small magnificence by the royal academy of sciences at Amsterdam. What it most resembles is a magpie's nest. With the rarest exceptions, all that it contains of any value, whether interpretation or illustration, is taken from others, and usually without acknowledgment. A reader new to the author and the editor might mistake van Wageningen for a man of learning; but with my knowledge of both I can trace every stolen penny to the pouch it came from. * * * From those of his predecessors who wrote in Latin he copies many whole sentences word for word, especially from Fayus and me. I am his chief resource in books I and III; my fourth volume appeared when his compilation was nearing completion and is therefore plundered less; in book II his wants were so abundantly supplied by the ampler and more elementary commentary of Mr Garrod that he left mine unread, only dipping into it here and there.

*   *   *   *   *   *

'Operam maximam eamque satis fastidiosam posui in primo emendationis cuiusque auctore inuestigando.' I am one of the few who can echo these words of Lachmann's: most editors have souls above such things, and some of them so much prefer error to knowledge that even when we patient drudges have ascertained the facts for them they continue to disseminate misinformation. There is another set of facts which I am almost alone in commemorating, for it is desired to suppress them. Many a reading discovered by conjecture has afterwards been confirmed by the authority of MSS.; and I record the occurrence, as instructive, instead of concealing it, as deplorable. The resistance of conservatives to true emendation is perpetual, and to enjoy credit in the future they must obliterate their past. When therefore a conjecture has turned out to be a manuscript reading, and they have gnashed their teeth and accepted it as such, they try to make the world forget that they formerly condemned it on its merits. Its author, who bore the blame of its supposed falsehood, is denied mention after the establishment of its truth; and the history of scholarship is mutilated to save the face of those who have impeded progress.

There is an industriously propagated legend that many of my own corrections are 'violent' or 'palaeographically improbable', by which it is merely meant that they alter a good number of letters. Violence and palaeographical improbability do not consist in that: they consist in ignoring the habits of copyists; and the terms should not be used by those to whom the habits of copyists are imperfectly known. A conjecture which alters only a single letter may be more improbable palaeographically than one which leaves no letter unaltered. * * *

The first virtue of an emendation is to be true; but the best emendations of all are those which are both true and difficult, emendations which no fool could find. It is humiliating to reflect how many of the type commonly called brilliant,—neat and pretty changes of a letter or two—, have been lighted upon, almost fortuitously, by scholars whose intellectual powers were beneath the ordinary. Textual criticism would indeed be a paradise if scribes had confined themselves to making mistakes which Isaac Voss and Robinson Ellis could correct. But we know by comparing one MS. with another that they also made mistakes of a different character; and it is these that put a good emendator on his mettle. First he must recognise them, then he must deal with them suitably. Anxious adherence to the *ductus litterarum* is the fruitful parent of false conjectures. It seduced even such men as Scaliger and Porson. * * * The merits essential to a correction are those without which it cannot be true, and closeness to the MSS. is not one of them; the indispensable things are fitness to the context and propriety to the genius of the author. The question whether the error presupposed was great or small is indeed a question to be asked, but it is the last question. With vulgar judges it is the first, though usually the last as well. This detail is their favourite criterion, because it can be discerned, or they think it can, by a bodily sense, without disturbing the slumbers of the intellect.

It surprises me that so many people should feel themselves qualified to weigh conjectures in their balance and to pronounce them good or bad, probable or improbable. Judging an emendation requires in some measure the same qualities as emendation itself, and the requirement is formidable. To read attentively, think correctly, omit no relevant consideration, and repress self-will, are not ordinary accomplishments; yet an emendator needs much besides: just literary perception, congenial intimacy with the author, experience which must have been won by study, and mother wit which he must have brought from his mother's womb.

It may be asked whether I think that I myself possess this outfit, or even most of it; and if I answer yes, that will be a new example of my notorious arrogance. I had rather be arrogant than impudent. I should not have undertaken to edit Manilius unless I had believed that I was fit for the task; and in particular I think myself a better judge of emendation, both when to emend and how to emend, than most others.

The following stanza of Mr de la Mare's 'Fare well' first met my eyes, thus printed, in a newspaper review.

> Oh, when this my dust surrenders
> Hand, foot, lip, to dust again,
> May these loved and loving faces
>   Please other men!
> May the rustling harvest hedgerow
> Still the Traveller's Joy entwine,
> And as happy children gather
>   Posies once mine.

I knew in a moment that Mr de la Mare had not written *rustling*, and in another moment I had found the true word. But if the book of poems had perished and the verse survived only in the review, who would have believed me rather than the compositor? The bulk of the reading public would have been perfectly content with *rustling*, nay they would sincerely have preferred it to the epithet which the poet chose. If I had been so ill-advised as to publish my emendation, I should have been told that *rustling* was exquisitely apt and poetical, because hedgerows do rustle, expecially in autumn, when the leaves are dry, and when straws and ears from the passing harvest-wain (to which 'harvest' is so plain an allusion that only a pedant like me could miss it) are hanging caught in the twigs; and I should have been recommended to quit my dusty (or musty) books and make a belated acquaintance with the sights and sounds of the English countryside. And the only possible answer would have been *ugh!*

My first reception was not worse than I expected. I provoked less enmity and insolence than Scaliger or Bentley in proportion as my merits were less eminent and unbearable than theirs. But my disregard of established opinions and my disrespect for contemporary fashions in scholarship made the ignorant feel sure that I was greatly and presumptuously in error and could be put down without much difficulty; and critiques were accordingly published which I do not suppose that their authors would now wish to rescue from oblivion. Not by paying any attention to any of them, not by swerving an inch from my original principles and practice, but by the mere act of living on and continuing to be the same, I have changed that state of things; and the deaf adder, though I can hardly say that she has unstopped her own ears, has begun to stifle her hisses for fear that they should reach the ears of posterity. Perhaps there will be no long posterity for learning; but the reader whose good opinion I desire and have done my utmost to secure is the next Bentley or Scaliger who may chance to occupy himself with Manilius.

3. JUVENAL (1905)[3]

A year ago I had no design of publishing or composing any such work as this. I knew indeed that the current texts of Juvenal, though praised in reviews and seemingly acceptable to readers, were neither well founded nor well constructed, and that this classic, like many more, had suffered some hurt from the reigning fashion of the hour, the fashion of leaning on one manuscript like Hope on her anchor and trusting to heaven that no harm will come of it. But I neither realised the extent of this injury nor fully understood its causes. I ascribed it first to the sloth and distaste for thinking which are the common inheritance of humanity, and secondly to that habit of treading in ruts and trooping in companies which men share with sheep. I did not know that it had also a third source, sheer ignorance of facts, and that the editors had left undone the first of all their duties and neglected to provide the author with an apparatus criticus.

In October 1903, having been asked by Mr Postgate to
undertake the recension of Juvenal for his *Corpus
Poetarum*, I began to gather from printed sources the
recorded variants; and I soon discovered that Juvenal's
modern editors were ignorant or regardless of even the
printed sources. I consulted the oldest MSS. in the British
Museum, but there was little to be learnt from these; so
returning to the published records I chose out seven
authorities which seemed to emerge above the crowd and
to possess some value of their own. Two of these, thanks to
Mr Hosius, were collated already; two were in England,
so I examined them myself; three were abroad, but of these
I procured enough knowledge for my purpose. Their
testimony, with that of the Viennese and other fragments,
I have added to the witness of our prime authority the
Pithoeanus; and I now present to the readers and especially
to the editors of Juvenal the first apparatus criticus which
they have ever seen.

*   *   *   *   *   *

The Pithoeanus was first applied to the recension of
Juvenal in 1585 by its godfather Petrus Pithoeus. His text,
founded on this MS., served in 1613 as a model to Rigaltius,
and Rigaltius served as a model to editors of Juvenal for
near two hundred years. From 1800 onward, when P had
long disappeared, Ruperti first, and then Achaintre and
Heinrich, produced recensions founded on inferior MSS.
But in the middle of the century the Pithoeanus was re-
discovered at Montpellier and was restored to its pride of
place by Otto Jahn and K. F. Hermann; and in the series
of modern editions, Jahn's of 1851, Hermann's of 1854,
Jahn's of 1868, Buecheler's of 1886 and 1893, the text of
Juvenal has drawn nearer and nearer to the text of P.

The tendency is not unbroken, for every one of the three editors deserts P in some places where the others follow it and follows it in some where they desert it; but the upshot is that our present vulgate,—Mr Buecheler's last edition and the very similar text on which Mr Friedlaender wrote his commentary of 1895,—stands closer to P than did any earlier recension.

What I propose to do is to arrest this current and turn it back. I shall not immediately succeed; for two things are necessary, of which I can furnish only one. The recension of Juvenal is now crippled not only by lack of knowledge but by lack of judgment; and though I can supply the editors with information which they have neglected to procure for themselves I cannot constrain them to make a prudent use of it. But under present circumstances no prudence would avail them much: they cannot now assess with justice the comparative value of P and of the other MSS., for the simple reason that they do not know, and do not even enquire, what those MSS. contain. * * * My work will enable the public, and will thus in a measure compel the editors, to employ their judgment, be it sound or crazy, upon facts. This is the first requisite, that the readings of the MSS. should be known. The second is that they should be treated, as they now are not, with impartiality.

What here follows is meant for one only of the three classes into whose hands this book will come. It is not for those who are critics: they know it already and will find it nothing but a string of truisms. It is not for those who never will be critics: they cannot grasp it and will find it nothing but a string of paradoxes. It is for beginners; for those who are not critics yet, but are neither too dull to learn nor too self-satisfied to wish to learn.

Open a modern recension of a classic, turn to the preface, and there you may almost count on finding, in Latin or German or English, some words like these: 'I have made it my rule to follow *a* wherever possible, and only where its readings are patently erroneous have I had recourse to *b* or *c* or *d*.' No scholar of eminence, even in the present age, has ever enunciated such a principle. Some, to be sure, like Mr Buecheler in his Juvenal, have virtually assumed it in their practice, as a convenient substitute for mental exertion; but to blurt it out as a maxim is an indiscretion which they leave to their unreflecting imitators, who formulate the rule without misgiving and practise it with conscious pride.

Either *a* is the source of *b* and *c* and *d* or it is not. If it is, then never in any case should recourse be had to *b* or *c* or *d*. If it is not, then the rule is irrational; for it involves the assumption that wherever *a*'s scribes made a mistake they produced an impossible reading. Three minutes' thought would suffice to find this out; but thought is irksome and three minutes is a long time.

How, you may ask, did the mind of man ever excogitate anything so false and foolish? The answer is that the mind of man had nothing to do with it. What the mind sets up the mind can pull down, and fancies based on false reasons can be overthrown by true reasons. But if true reasons could overthrow this fancy it would have been overthrown long before our time; by Madvig for instance in *Opusc.* II, pp. 298–319. Its strength is that it has no reasons, only causes. Its root is not in the mind but in the soul; and it partakes the solidity of its indestructible foundations, the sloth and vanity of man.

The task of editing the classics is continually attempted by scholars who have neither enough intellect nor enough literature. Unless a false reading chances to be unmetrical or ungrammatical they have no means of knowing that it is false. Show them these variants,

$$\text{molliaque} \begin{Bmatrix} \text{inmittens} \\ \text{inmites} \end{Bmatrix} \text{fixit in ora manus,}$$

and they cannot tell which is right and which is wrong; and, what is worse, they honestly believe that nobody else can tell. If you suppose yourself able to distinguish a true reading from a false one,—suppose yourself, that is, to be a critic, a man capable of doing what the Greeks called κρίνειν,—they are aghast at your assurance. I am aghast at theirs: at the assurance of men who do not even imagine themselves to be critics, and yet presume to meddle with criticism.

What a critic is, and what advantage he has over those who are not critics, can easily be shown by one example. Cicero's oration *Pro rege Deiotaro* was edited between 1830 and 1840 by Klotz, Soldan, and Benecke. The best MS. then known was the Erfurtensis, and all three editors pounced on this authority and clung to it, believing themselves safe. Madvig in 1841, maintaining reason against superstition in Cicero's text as I now maintain it in Juvenal's, impugned 17 readings adopted from the Erfurtensis by these editors, and upheld the readings of inferior MSS. We now possess MSS. still better than the Erfurtensis, and in 12 of the 17 places they contradict it; they confirm the inferior MSS. and the superior critic. Authority itself has crossed over to the side of reason and left superstition in the lurch.

But there are editors destitute of this discriminating faculty, so destitute that they cannot even conceive it to exist; and these are entangled in a task for which nature has neglected to equip them. What are they now to do? Set to and try to learn their trade? that is forbidden by sloth. Stand back and leave room for their superiors?

that is forbidden by vanity. They must have a rule, a machine to do their thinking for them. If the rule is true, so much the better; if false, that cannot be helped: but one thing is necessary, a rule.

A hundred years ago it was their rule to count the MSS. and trust the majority. But this pillow was snatched from under them by the great critics of the 19th century, and the truth that MSS. must be weighed, not counted, is now too widely known to be ignored. The sluggard has lost his pillow, but he has kept his nature, and must needs find something else to loll on; so he fabricates, to suit the change of season, his precious precept of following one MS. wherever possible. Engendered by infirmity and designed for comfort, no wonder if it misses the truth at which it was never aimed. Its aim was purely humanitarian: to rescue incompetent editors alike from the toil of editing and from the shame of acknowledging that they cannot edit.

Frailty of understanding is in itself no proper target for scorn and mockery: 'nihil in eo odio dignum, misericordia digna multa.' But the unintelligent forfeit their claim to compassion when they begin to indulge in self-complacent airs, and to call themselves sane critics, meaning that they are mechanics. And when, relying upon their numbers, they pass from self-complacency to insolence, and reprove their betters for using the brains which God has not denied them, they dry up the fount of pity. 'D'où vient' asks Pascal 'qu'un boiteux ne nous irrite pas, et qu'un esprit boiteux nous irrite? C'est à cause qu'un boiteux reconnoit que nous allons droit, et qu'un esprit boiteux dit que c'est nous qui boitons; sans cela nous en aurions plus de pitié que de colère.' If a hale man walks along the street upon two sound legs, he is not liable to be chased by crowds of cripples vociferating 'Go home and fetch your crutch'. If a reasoning man edits a classic rationally, he is.

When the Pithoeanus has one reading and other MSS. another, and it is sought to determine which reading, if either, is true, then, if a critic attempts to settle the question, as critics will, by pertinent considerations, considerations of sense or usage or palaeography, he is exposed to a form of molestation from which the students of other sciences are probably exempt. He is pretty sure to be told that the judgment of critics is fallible, which he knew already, and that he ought to follow the authority of the best MS. P. Now ask the intermeddler a question which he has never asked himself. Whence comes authority? In what does the goodness of a MS. consist, and upon what does our belief in its goodness repose? If any one has heard a voice from heaven saying 'P is the best MS. of Juvenal', let him take example by M. Caedicius and carry his tale to the magistrates. But if not, then the goodness of a MS. consists simply and solely in the goodness of the readings which it proffers; and our belief in its goodness, that is to say in the goodness of its readings, reposes simply and solely upon our judgment: upon that same judgment which we are now forbidden to exercise. When you invoke the authority of a MS. against the exercise of the judgment, you are inciting the creature to rebel against the creator, and you are sapping the very ground on which you stand. If nobody can tell a true reading from a false reading, it follows of necessity that nobody can tell a truthful MS. from a lying MS. Continue then, if you like, to urge that the judgment of critics is fallible, as indeed it is; but desist from talking in the same breath about the superiority of one MS. to another; for this phrase either means nothing at all, or else it means that the one MS. has been placed above the other by the fallible judgment of critics.

Take another aspect of the case. If a student, desiring to find out whether Pindar was stupid or no, should begin

to read him, would any one touch him on the shoulder and
say 'Shut that book: Boeotians were stupid, Pindar was
a Boeotian, therefore Pindar was stupid'? No, not even
a 'sane critic': even he reserves such reasoning for his own
ghostly realm of make-believe, and does not carry it into
the waking world where men pursue their business in the
daylight and detect *petitio principii*. Whether Boeotians were
stupid, and to what extent, can only be settled by considering on its intrinsic merits the case of every known Boeotian,
and Pindar's case among the rest. And whether P is the
best MS. of Juvenal, and to what extent, can only be
settled by considering on its intrinsic merits every discrepancy between P and the other MSS. If, while we are
engaged in so considering one of these discrepancies, you
interrupt us with the assertion, possibly quite true, that P
is the best MS. and far the best, we shall reply: 'That is the
question which we are now investigating at a preliminary
stage. When we have made up our minds about this
passage, then we will add it either to the evidence in
favour of P or else to the evidence in favour of Ψ. To warp
our choice in this particular instance by assuming as
proved the general conclusion for which we are now collect-
ing materials is, in the full sense of the term, preposterous.'

The truth is that when these gentlemen talk about the
authority of better MSS. they are repeating at second hand
a phrase which they have caught up and run away with.
They have overheard critics using it, but what the critics
meant by it they do not understand. There is a sphere,
a narrow sphere, within which the authority of better
MSS. is properly and usefully invoked, not indeed as a
good means of arriving at the truth, but as the best means
available. I 2 'rauci Theseide *Cordi*' P, *Codri* Ψ: the man's
name is unknown. I 21 'sit uacat *ac* placidi rationem
admittitis' P, *et* Ψ: there is not a pin to choose. I 134

'*caulis* miseris atque ignis emendus' P, *caules* Ψ: the
singular is no better than the plural nor the plural than
the singular. To decide what Juvenal wrote in these places
the judgment is helpless: here then we avail ourselves of
an instrument which the judgment has forged and put into
our hands: our knowledge or opinion of the relative merits
of the MSS. Since we have found P the most trustworthy
MS. in places where its fidelity can be tested, we infer
that it is also the most trustworthy in places where no test
can be applied; and we read *Cordi, ac, caulis*. In thus
committing ourselves to the guidance of the best MS. we
cherish no hope that it will always lead us right: we know
that it will often lead us wrong; but we know that any
other MS. would lead us wrong still oftener. By following
any other MS. we shall only be right in the minority of
cases; by following P we shall be right in the majority:
that is all we look for. A critic therefore, when he employs
this method of trusting the best MS., employs it in the
same spirit of gloomy resignation with which a man lies
down on a stretcher when he has broken both his legs.
But far other is the spirit in which it is hailed by the
reciter of formulas. He is not dejected by its inadequacy,
but captivated by its ease. 'Here' says he 'is a method,
sanctioned by critics, employed in scientific enquiry, and
yet involving not the slightest expenditure of intellectual
effort: this is the method for me'; and he espouses it for
ever. In places where critics rise up and walk, where
judgment has scope and authority is superseded, he remains supine and marvels at the vagaries of pedestrians:
presumptuous beings who expect to reach their goal by
the capricious and arbitrary method of putting forward
first one foot, and then, with strange inconsistency, the
other.

Misfortunes never come single, and the prattlers about

P's authority are afflicted not only with lack of understanding but with loss of memory. They forget that they
themselves repeatedly do what they say that we ought
not to do; repeatedly prefer their own judgment to the
authority of the Pithoeanus. The Pithoeanus at 1 35 omits
the word *palpat*, but they will not omit it; at 1 38 it reads
non tibi, but they will read *noctibus*: they will follow the
worse MSS. instead of the best. For deserting the
Pithoeanus then they cannot blame us, since in that
action we agree with them: they must blame us for the
feature in which our conduct differs from theirs. Our
offence is that we do not desert the Pithoeanus in the proper
spirit, the spirit of rats leaving a sinking ship. We quit
the best MS. in search of truth: we ought only to quit it,
as they do, in search of shelter. In enquiring whether a
given reading of P's is right, we behave as if we really
wanted to know, and we ask whether it is probable: they
ask only whether it is possible, and unless it is impossible
they believe it to be right: much as if you should believe
that every Irishman is a Roman Catholic unless he knocks
you down for looking as if you thought so.

REVIEWS, CLASSICAL PAPERS
AND LETTERS TO THE PRESS

The following pieces, which for the most part are extracts only, were contributed to the 'Classical Review', the 'Journal of Philology', the 'Classical Quarterly', and the 'Cambridge Review', between 1890 and 1923. The two letters are of later date.

1. TUCKER'S 'SUPPLICES' OF AESCHYLUS (1890)[1]

THIS edition gives proof of many virtues: common sense, alert perception, lucidity of thought, impatience of absurdity, a rational distrust of MS. tradition, and a masculine taste in things poetical. The learner who attacks the play with this commentary will find unfailing help by the way and acquire much information before his journey's end. The old miserable experiences of the classical student who wants to understand what he reads, his lonely fights with difficulties whose presence the editor has never apprehended, his fruitless quest of a meaning in notes where the editor has rendered Greek nonsense into English nonsense and gone on his way rejoicing, are not repeated here. Here on the contrary is a commentator who shares the reader's difficulties, rescues him from some of them, warns him of some existing unperceived, and to tell the truth invents a good many where none exist.

It is Prof. Tucker's main concern, as it must be for an editor of this play, to find out what Aeschylus wrote; and his administration of this province will decide the value of the book as an original contribution to learning. He has introduced into the text, I reckon roughly, about 200 conjectures of his own. It is the critic's chief duty, and should be his chief pleasure, to commend what is good; so I begin with four emendations which I should call quite certain. * * *

Among the residue of the 200 conjectures there may very well be some which will seem more probable to other critics than to me, but there can hardly be many. * * * What vitiates two thirds of Mr Tucker's conjectures is that despite his professions he takes no due heed to palaeographical probability. 'In the present work,' says he in his preface, 'there have been assumed as axioms...(iii) that the reading substituted on conjecture must approve its claims by satisfying the conditions of palaeography—as a most natural source of the incorrect reading.' But this is just what an average conjecture of Mr Tucker's does not. True, it seldom sets the MS. utterly at naught, and it is usually fortified by a parade of uncial type, the decorative effect of which is often pleasing; but it diverges too far from the *ductus litterarum* to have any convincing force. Possible no doubt it is; but half-a-dozen alternatives are equally possible. We know of course that the scribes did make mistakes as bad as those which Mr Tucker postulates; but when such mistakes have once been made they can never be corrected. * * *

When Mr Tucker's conjectures are not palaeographically improbable they are apt to be causeless and even detrimental. Among the axioms assumed in the preface are the following: 'the reading in the text must hold its place until such cause to the contrary can be shewn as will satisfy a rigidly impartial tribunal. The *onus probandi* lies entirely with the impugner of the text.' 'The conditions of dispossession are these. It must either be proved that the reading is an impossibility, or else that in point of grammar it is so abnormal, or in point of relevance so manifestly inappropriate, as to produce a thorough conviction that the MS. is in error.' I for my part should call this much too strict; but these are Mr Tucker's principles. His practice is something quite different: in practice no word, however good, is safe if Mr Tucker can think of a similar word which is not much worse. * * *

The emendations of scholars fare no better than the readings of the MS. if their place is wanted for a conjecture of the editor's own. Again and again in passages which we all thought had been corrected long ago Mr Tucker proffers another solution, not better but newer, and promotes it, with rigid partiality, to the text. * * *

Here I have given proofs enough of the disasters which attend us when we desist from the pursuit of truth to follow after our own inventions. Thus much it was necessary to say, because the many students who will I hope resort to this edition for help and instruction must be warned that they will find not only what they seek but also a good deal which they are not to believe. The book however in spite of its faults is the most useful edition of the *Supplices* we have. The purely explanatory part of the commentary does not contain very much that is absolutely new, and this is well; for it is really a far more venturesome thing, if critics would but understand it, to propose a new rendering than a new reading. * * *

The translation is written with vigour and adroitness, and its rhythm is often admirable.

2. THE MANUSCRIPTS OF PROPERTIUS (1892, 1894)[2]

In the year 1816 Karl Lachmann published at Leipzig the first scientific recension of Propertius. As for the textual criticism of his predecessors it resembled nothing so much as the condition of mankind before the advent of Prometheus: ἔφυρον εἰκῆ πάντα. The younger Burmann's great edition of 1780 presents an imperfect and inaccurate collation of some five and twenty MSS. good and bad and indifferent: the authority for this reading or that, if reckoned at all, is ascertained by the simple process of adding up the codices which offer it: if one MS. weighs heavier than its fellows, that is because it has had the luck to be collated twice over under the different names of Mentelianus and Leidensis primus and accordingly counts as two. To the conjectural emendation of the text the critics of the 17th and 18th centuries rendered immortal services; two of them at least, Heinsius and Schrader, achieved in this province far more than Lachmann: but towards the formation of a critical apparatus they did nothing but amass a chaos of material and leave it to be set in order by this young man of twenty-three.

Lachmann singled out from the crowd of witnesses the codices Groninganus and Neapolitanus and made these two the pillars of his recension: the Groninganus he reckoned first in merit, the Neapolitanus second, the other MSS. he employed but sparingly or discarded altogether. He did well—I will here assume as proven what I shall prove hereafter—to select the Neapolitanus, which remains today an authority second to none: he did well also to select the Groninganus, which though now superseded contains nevertheless much truth which the Neapolitanus does not contain. He erred, though the error was of no great

moment, in setting the Groninganus highest, misled by
specious interpolations which he mistook for genuine: he
erred more gravely and disastrously in neglecting the MS.
known to him as the alter codex Burmanni and to us as the
Dauentriensis, whose honest and independent witness he
mistook for interpolation.

Lachmann's right opinions had the strength of truth;
his wrong opinions were sustained by his genius and grow-
ing authority; right and wrong together they took captive
the learned world and held sway unchallenged till 1843.
Keil in that year published his *Observationes criticae in
Propertium* and there corrected Lachmann's less important
error by demonstrating that the Neapolitanus must be set
at least on a level with the Groninganus. Hertzberg,
whose elaborate edition was then in publication, still held
wholly with Lachmann; but from this date onward the
Neapolitanus gained more and more in honour as the
Groninganus lost, and the chief critics and editors down
to 1880, as Haupt, Mueller and Palmer, took N for their
mainstay and made but subsidiary use of the Groninganus
or of any MS. beside.

But 1880 like 1816 began a new era. In this year the
late Emil Baehrens published a recension founded on four
MSS., two of them, A and D, already known in part from
Burmann's edition under the names of Vossianus secundus
and alter codex meus, two now first collated, F and V.
From these four alone, A and F forming one family, D and
V another, Baehrens proposed to reconstitute the archetype: all other MSS., N included, were to be set aside, and
their testimony, where it dissented from AFDV, was to be
deemed interpolated.

The edition of Baehrens placed in our hands all the
materials for restoring the text of Propertius which are
yet known to exist: that he himself should not employ

them rightly was excusable enough, since men are apt to be overmuch enamoured of their own discoveries. His four MSS. were really of high importance and superseded not only the Groninganus but all known MSS. excepting N; N however they did not supersede, and Baehrens was further mistaken in ascribing to interpolators certain readings, often agreeing with N, which are offered by f and v the correctors of F and V. Somewhere, it might have been thought, in the world of scholarship there would be found the candour and the perspicacity to welcome his distinguished services, correct his demonstrable mistakes, and establish without more ado on a sure foundation the textual criticism of Propertius.

But Baehrens was envied for his talents and disliked for his vanity and arrogance; many of his contemporaries, not all of whom deserved it, he had assailed with abuse; and by his lack of due servility towards the deified heroes Lachmann and Haupt he had affronted the school of philologers now regnant in Germany. Accordingly it was not to be borne that valuable MSS. unknown to Haupt or Lachmann should be discovered by Baehrens; and the task of proving that his MSS. were valueless was promptly undertaken in the *Rheinisches Museum* of the same year 1880, vol. xxxv, pp. 441–7, by Mr Friedrich Leo. Mr Leo is known from his services to Plautus and Seneca for a very competent critic; but Baehrens two years before had described him with foolish scurrility as an 'asinus sub Leonina pelle'.†

Mr Leo successfully demonstrated that in discarding the Neapolitanus Baehrens erred: his proofs are not invariably cogent and we shall see hereafter that they can be largely reinforced, but they sufficed. This however was not enough;

† Haec prius fuere: in 1891 Mr Leo on p. 21 of his edition of the *Culex* writes kindly and justly of Baehrens.

and having corrected the error of Baehrens Mr Leo must next proceed to put himself no less in the wrong by asserting, not proving, for that was impossible, that 'AFDV omnino nihil ualent', and returning to the rubbish-heap of old MS. materials superseded by Baehrens' discoveries. Into the relationship of the MSS. to one another he made no investigation, and indeed he could hardly have made any without upsetting his conclusion.

A few months later Mr Ellis published in the *American Journal of Philology*, vol. 1, pp. 389–400, a paper on 'the Neapolitanus of Propertius'. Considered as a defence of that MS. the article was by no means equal to Mr Leo's in completeness, method or precision; but it was quite untouched by faction or prejudice, and the author was content to vindicate N without disparaging AFDV. Like Mr Leo he held that certain of the vulgar codices were not yet superseded, and like Mr Leo he propounded no theory of the relations existing between the MSS.

In 1882 appeared the most elaborate work yet published on the subject, a dissertation *De codicibus Propertianis* by Mr Richard Solbisky of Weimar. Rightly ignoring all MSS. but N and AFDV Mr Solbisky addressed himself to comparing the merits and defining the relations of these. He concluded that for practical purposes N and the family DV are our only authorities, both necessary but N the better of the two: the family AF may be set down as useless. The MSS. are related thus: N descends from one apograph of the archetype, the family DV from another; the family AF is blent from both these apographs and contains no other element of genuine tradition but only errors and interpolations with a few happy conjectures; f and v have derived readings from a MS. resembling N. The treatise is written with admirable diligence, adequate learning and entire freedom from the spirit of faction: its faults spring partly from a deficiency, I will not say in critical faculty, but certainly in critical experience; partly, it seems, from the fact that though party spirit is absent preconceived opinion is not. One finds conclusions, correct in themselves, supported by proofs which prove nothing; false or doubtful propositions are stated as self-evident; the codices AF are disparaged in a manner not only erroneous but arbitrary; and for his genealogy of the MSS., which I shall shew to be quite impossible, Mr Solbisky neither adduces nor pretends to adduce any evidence at all.

The *Études critiques sur Properce* of Mr Frédéric Plessis published in 1884 contain two chapters, pp. 1–45, devoted to the MSS. The book is written with French lucidity and more than French diligence; but Mr Plessis, it must be said, is no critic. His conclusions, which since he shews no argument for them appear to be intuitive, are these: the MSS. to be employed in constructing the text are NAFDV, the Groninganus and Hertzberg's Hamburgensis: there are two families: the first comprises two branches of which N is the better and AF the worse: the second family consists of DV and is inferior to N but equal to AF. f and v derive from N the readings which they have in common with that MS.: Mr Plessis, who as I have said is no critic, adds that the agreement of Nfv 'équivaut presque à une certitude', i.e. a reading found in N is rendered more probable if two scribes have copied it thence. The Groninganus and Hamburgensis have combined the readings of the two families already mentioned, but are nevertheless to be employed in constructing the text.

In 1887 Mr C. Weber published a disquisition *De auctoritate codicum Propertianorum* in which after a painstaking examination confined to the first book he came to the following conclusions: N is by far our best authority but AFDV with f and v are also of service: of the two families AF and DV the former is akin to N but the latter is nevertheless the better: f and v derived readings from a MS. resembling N but interpolated. Mr Weber's conclusions then, so far as they concern the relations of NAFDV, are virtually those of Mr Plessis. * * *

Controversy is inseparable from the discussion of our subject, and the ensuing pages will of necessity contain a certain amount of polemical matter; but my purpose is not in the main controversial. My purpose is to establish my own theory: to demolish the theories of others is only a necessary incident in the process. Therefore I shall not examine point by point the conclusions of my predecessors and controvert them severally: I shall develop my own views in what appears to be the most natural sequence, pointing out from time to time how this or that error of former critics is refuted by the evidence adduced.

The mass of facts which I am about to pass in review is much greater than would be needed merely to demonstrate the thesis which I have proposed. But side by side with the demonstration of my thesis I pursue a second aim: to amend or elucidate as far as may be those passages in our author where his MSS. are not unanimous and where it becomes our business to extract from their conflicting testimony the reading of the Propertian archetype.

* * * * * *

(1894) To conclude: I design this treatise for a defence of eclecticism, but of eclecticism within scientific bounds. The student of an ancient text has two enemies. There is the devotee of system who prefers simplicity to truth, and who having half learnt from Madvig and Bekker the great lesson of our century, 'magnam et inconditam testium

turbam ad paucos et certos esse redigendam, a quibus
ceteri rem acceperint', selects his few witnesses without
ascertaining if they were really the informants of the rest,
constructs a neat apparatus at whatever cost to the text of
his hapless author, and seeks to overawe the timid by
sonorous talk about 'sanae artis praecepta omnia'; and
there is the born hater of science who ransacks Europe for
waste paper that he may fill his pages to half their height
with the lees of the Italian renascence, and then by appeals
to the reader's superstition would persuade him to hope
without reason and against likelihood that he will gather
grapes of thorns and figs of thistles. Here is my attempt
to fortify against delusion on either hand the student of at
least one Latin author.

3. SCHULZE'S EDITION OF BAEHRENS' CATULLUS[3]
This review, of 1894, is printed in full.

The first edition of Baehrens' Catullus, which now that
the second has appeared will fetch fancy prices, was in
the rigour of the term an epoch-making work. But it
exhibited a text of the author much corrupted by un-
provoked or unlikely or incredible conjecture; so that the
task of revision was delicate, and the choice of a reviser
was not easy. It was not easy; but scholars who are acquainted with the history of Catullus' text and with the
metres he wrote in, who know how to edit a book and how
to collate a manuscript, who are capable of coherent
reasoning or at all events of consecutive thought, exist;
and to such a scholar the task might have been allotted.
    It has been allotted to Mr Schulze, who says, 'Munus
nouae huius libelli editionis post praematuram Aemilii
Baehrensii mortem curandae ita suscepi, ut quoad fieri

posset quam plurima eorum, quae ille ad Catulli carmina et recensenda et emendanda contulisset, retinerem ac seruarem.' Out of Baehrens' conjectures Mr Schulze has found it possible to retain six. The first of these is the merely orthographical correction 2 6 *lubet* for *libet* or *iubet*. Two more are specimens of Baehrens' most despicable trifling: 6 9 *heic et illeic*† for *hec et illo*, as if forsooth that were a less and not a greater change than the old *hic et ille*; and 21 13 *nei* for *nec* instead of the usual *ne*, as if *nec* were not a perpetual corruption of *ne* in the MSS. of authors who never wrote *nei* in their lives. The three others, 68 139 *concipit*, 100 6 *egregie est*, 111 2 *ex nimiis*, are somewhat above the low average of Baehrens' conjectures.

But the emendations which place Baehrens next to Haupt among the post-Lachmannian correctors of Catullus are the things which Mr Schulze has not found it possible to retain. Take for shortness' sake the 64th poem only. I will not be unreasonable and complain that Mr Schulze omits Baehrens' correction of v. 73 *illa ex tempestate ferox quo tempore*; because I know that Mr Schulze has never seen or heard of that correction. It occurs in Baehrens' commentary, and Mr Schulze has not read Baehrens' commentary. That I affirm securely: if you ask 'whence then did Mr Schulze learn (p. 97) that Baehrens had proposed *prompta* at 68 39?' I reply that he learnt it from Schwabe's edition of 1886; and if you ask 'how does he know (p. v) that Baehrens abandoned in the commentary some of his earlier conjectures?' I reply that he knows it from Iwan Mueller's *Jahresbericht*. For if he had read the commentary he would not merely know that Baehrens abandoned some conjectures but he would know which those conjectures are; and he does not. He still represents

† The text has *illei*, whether from a misprint or from an improvement of Mr Schulze's.

Baehrens as proposing *quaecumueis* at 64 109, though Baehrens in the commentary said 'quam formam minime latinam non debui olim exemplis male fidis deceptus recipere'. And this barbarous and repudiated depravation, and the frivolous *heic* at 269, are all of Baehrens that Mr Schulze finds it possible even to mention within the 400 verses of the 64th poem. The transposition of 216 and 217, *nascente* in 275, *incultum cano...crinem* in 350, *residens* in 387, *Amarunsia* in 395,—these may be found at least recorded in the editions of other scholars, but not in this book which bears on its front 'recensuit Aemilius Baehrens'. The transposition is accepted both by Riese and by Postgate, the emendation of 350 by Riese, Postgate and Schwabe, the emendation of 387 is approved by Schwabe and accepted by Riese and Schmidt: but no vestige of these corrections survives in the monument reared to their author's memory by the Oedipodean piety of Mr Schulze.†

Baehrens' are not the only emendations which Mr Schulze finds it impossible to retain or even to record. Which is the finest correction ever made in Catullus I will not undertake to say; but one of the first half-dozen is Froelich's 'non est sana puella nec rogare | qualis sit solet *aes* [*et* MSS.] imaginosum', which Baehrens of course accepted. Mr Schulze ousts it for 'nec *rogate* | qualis sit *solide est imaginosa*'. But no reader is likely to waste a glance on these Berlin goods if Froelich's restoration is left glittering in the apparatus criticus; so Mr Schulze does not leave it there: he suppresses it. *Quaecumque adeo possunt afferre pudorem*, says Ovid, *illa tegi caeca condita nocte decet*.

One clue Mr Schulze appears to possess; if he sees the name of Lachmann he follows it, 'errabunda regens tenui uestigia filo'. I say advisedly *the name*. At 63 5 he expels

† 'Tam bene de poeta suo meruit, ut dignus sit, cuius memoria pie colatur,' p. v.

the emendations of Auantius and Bergk and writes 'deuol-sit *ile*': it is not sense, but it is Lachmann's. A still more pleasing instance of simple faith occurs at 63 74 where Mr Schulze reads with Lachmann 'roseis ut huic labellis sonitus abiit *celer*'. Lachmann himself, 'uir egregius' as Haupt calls him 'et multo quam imbecilli capiunt maior', had a reason for adding *celer*: his theory of the pagination of the archetype made this verse the 18th line on the 41st page, while the 18th line on the 39th page was 'aliena quae petentes velut exules loca *celeri*,' whence he took the hypermetrical word to repair the deficiency here. But Mr Schulze does not hold Lachmann's theory, for on p. lxiv he retains a note of Baehrens' which says 'tota ista numerorum singularum in V paginarum paginarumque uersuum computatio a Lachmanno instituta et ab Hauptio [quaest. Cat. p. 39–49; op. I 28 sq.] multis defensa ad nihilum recidit'; nor is it through inadvertence that he retains this note, for he has taken the trouble to write 'ab Hauptio' where Baehrens wrote 'a Hauptio' and to add the reference to the opuscula. He has abandoned then the basis of Lachmann's conjecture, but to the conjecture he adheres; and why not? its merit is not that he thinks it has a basis but that he knows it is Lachmann's. Again, when Lachmann has emended a passage, Mr Schulze allows no one to improve Lachmann's emendation, because he does not know whether the improvement is an im-provement and he does know that it is not Lachmann's. At 66 58 the MSS. have '*gratia* Canopieis incola litoribus', Lachmann emended *Graia*, and Baehrens improved this to *Graiia*, which Lachmann of course would have adopted, as any one can see who turns to his note on Lucr. i 477 or remembers, as Haupt says, 'quotiens ex antiquae scri-bendi consuetudinis recordatione maxime Lachmannus in Catulli carminibus fructum ceperit'. But no painting of the lily for Mr Schulze, who ejects *Graiia* and replaces *Graia* in the text. I do not know all the salutations with which his idol will hereafter welcome him to Elysium, nor durst I write them down if I did; but from what happened to Eichstaedt and Forbiger I can tell that *mancipium* and *simius* are two of them. At the end of the note however Mr Schulze ventures on a suggestion of his own: 'fortasse *grata*.' It is news then to this editor of Catullus that for 300 years no text was printed with any other reading than *grata*: history for him begins with 1829: he supposes Scaliger and Heinsius and Bentley and the rest of them went on content with *gratia* till Lachmann came upon earth to tell mankind that it was a trisyllable.

This brings us to Mr Schulze's own emendations. One of these, *monendum est te* for *monendum est* at 39 9, is no worse than the *monendum te est* and *monendus es* of others, so that the odds against it are only two to one. Then in several places he writes *uoster* where the MSS. are divided between *uester* and *noster*. Catullus may of course have used that form, but this divergency of the MSS. affords not the slightest ground for thinking that he did: *uester* and *noster* are interchanged not in his text only, but in all authors whose MSS. are medieval; and they are interchanged not because those authors wrote *uoster* but from the cause exhibited in Mr Schulze's own note at 71 3: 'u̅r̅m̅ VM: n̅r̅m̅ g.' At 10 25 *sqq.* Mr Schulze punctuates 'quaeso, inquit, mihi, mi Catulle, paulum | istos: commoda nam uolo ad Serapim | deferri', but omits to say whether this means 'I wish my emoluments to be carried to Serapis' or 'I wish to be carried to Serapis in an obliging frame of mind'. Finally he emends 29 20 thus:

hunc Galliae timent, timet Britannia.

Two metrical solecisms in one line.

Baehrens' spelling, which was bad, Mr Schulze has corrected as well as he knows how. He knows how to spell *sicine nequiquam* and *condicio*; so these words are rightly spelt. He does not know how to spell *umidus iucundus sodalicium* or *multa*; these words therefore retain their Baehrensian forms.

Baehrens' apparatus criticus was, as usual, a model of lucidity and order. Take a few examples of what it now is. At 68 140 the text has 'noscens omniuoli plurima furta Iouis,' where 'furta' is an old and generally accepted correction for the 'facta' of the MSS. An editor who knows his trade expresses this fact by writing 'furta *uulgo*, facta V'. Mr Schulze's note is 'plurima facta VM plurima furta *uulgo*': to occupy the printer he writes 'plurima' twice where it ought not to be written at all; to delay the reader he puts the note wrong end foremost. At 113 2 is a still wilder scene: text, 'Maeciliam: facto consule nunc iterum': note of a competent workman, 'Maeciliam *Lachmannus*, Meciliā G, Mecilia O, Maecilia *uulgo*, Mucillam *Pleitnerus*': note of Mr Schulze, 'Mecilia OM Meciliā G | facto VM | Maecilia: facto *uulgo* Maeciliam: facto *Lachmannus* Mucillam: facto *Pleitnerus*.' Another revelation of the amateur encounters us in such places as 64 386: the text is 'saepe pater diuum templo in fulgente reuisens', which is the MS. reading, so that of course there should be no note at all unless some conjecture is to be mentioned: Mr Schulze writes 'reuisens VM.' Why not 'saepe VM, pater VM, diuum VM, templo VM, in VM, fulgente VM'? Elsewhere Mr Schulze's ignorance of how things are done and inability to learn have made his notes completely unintelligible, and a reader who wants to know what the MSS. give must consult another edition. Take 61 46 *sq*.: text, 'quis deus magis est ama-|tis petendus amantibus': note, 'amatis VM magis a magis *Scaliger* ancxiis *Hauptius*

magis est ama-tis *Bergkius*': problem, what is the MS.
reading? From other editions you learn that it is 'magis
amatis est.' These are the sights which may now be seen
in what was once the apparatus criticus of Baehrens: for
appropriate comments I refer the reader to Cic. *Phil.* ii
c. 41.

Now for the prolegomena. The prolegomena, I need not
say, were the kernel of Baehrens' edition. In them he
demonstrated, what no one suspected before but every one
acknowledges now, that the Oxoniensis (O) and the
Sangermanensis (G) are the authorities on which the text
of Catullus rests. All that is now in dispute is whether the
other MSS. are quite useless, as Baehrens held, or only
almost useless, as his opponents hold. His prolegomena are
thus the chief landmark in the criticism of Catullus' MSS.,
and there were two reasons why they should have been
kept intact: their intrinsic merit, and their historical
interest. Errors they may contain; and Bentley's Horace
and Lachmann's Lucretius contain errors, but Mr Schulze
has not yet been invited to revise those works.

Baehrens held that G and O are the only copies ever
made of the lost archetype V, and that the other MSS.
(ς) are all derived from G. His disputation ran as follows.
When G and O disagree, ς almost always side with G;
and they side with it not only in corruptions but in false
conjectures which its corrector has introduced and which
they cannot have got from any ancient MS.: therefore ς
are derived from G. On the other hand all ς, or nearly all,
often agree in one reading when G and O agree in another:
therefore ς, except perhaps the Datanus, are not derived
straight from G but from an apograph of G containing
conjectures. The few instances where ς agree with O
against G are partly due to true conjectures in this apograph, partly, where the difference is very minute, to

accident: the Santenianus (L) has marginal readings taken from O, but whether O was ever transcribed entire he doubts. Where G and O and ς all three differ, the reading of ς is conjectural. As to the Datanus (D), which has at least one interpolation from Thomas Seneca, none of its readings (*posquam*, *demostres*, etc.) are necessarily genuine but may be sham-antique: sometimes, like almost all other MSS., it gives better readings than GO, but these are conjectures: it is so interpolated that he does not trouble to decide whether it comes straight from G or through the same apograph as the others, for from G it comes: else why does it agree with G in error where O preserves the truth, and why, above all, does it reproduce almost every reading of G's corrector? questions which also apply to the rest of ς. He then discusses the marginal variants found in G: these must have been in the archetype because the scribe of G says he had only one exemplar: many of them appear in ς, which shows that they had most of them been copied into the apograph of G from which ς are derived.

Baehren's arguments are now expunged, and in their place stands printed matter composed by Mr Schulze. He sets out to demonstrate that all our MSS. come from a single codex, and fills more than two pages with passages which prove, or do not prove (the very first is 'I 5 *est* pro *es* codd. omnes sinceri' where of course 'sinceri' just begs the question), what might have been proved in two lines: I notice that this form of exercise is now much in vogue with amateurs who wish to be critics and think this is the way. The archetype, he holds, was four times transcribed: one transcript is O, another G: 'librorum OG praestantiam magnus numerus locorum ostendit, quibus *soli* [my italics] ueram lectionem aut certe meliorem quam ceteri *omnes* [mine again] codices praebent.' The list begins 'I 9 *quod* OG ς plerique: *quidem* ς complures', and contains '42 22 *nobis* OG ς plerique: *uobis* ς pauci' and '61 100 *uolet* OG ς plerique: *nolet* D, *nollet* AL': Mr Schulze is proving what is indisputably true and denied by nobody, and yonder is how he proves it. Then follow a number of places where ς agree with g (*i.e.* the corrector of G) in opposition to OG, and then (p. xliii) these incredible words: 'uel hac re eorum opinio refutatur, qui, ut Baehrensius et qui eum secuti sunt, omnes ς ex G fluxisse opinentur. nam cum codd. ς saepe cum G facere supra uideremus, qua re illi ut ς ex G descriptos esse putarent inducti sunt, hic non minorem numerum locorum congessimus, quibus ς cum g consentiunt.' And pray what is g? simply the corrector of G: the fact then that ς agree with the corrections found in G proves that Baehrens was wrong in supposing ς to be derived from G! This is no malevolent fiction of mine: it is what Mr Schulze has written and Messrs Teubner printed. But in the next sentence Mr Schulze faintly remembers what g is, so he says that if the corrections in G are derived, as he holds, from some lost copy of the archetype, 'manifestum est fieri potuisse ut etiam ς non ex G, sed ex eodem illo codice correcto fluerent': *fieri potuisse*! so evaporates our refutation of Baehrens. 'Atque adeo g ς inter se conspirant, ut ex eodem codice interpolato descripti esse uideantur': yes, and Abraham and Isaac were so much alike that they appear to have been brothers.

Next we have places where ς agree with OG against g; then 'Og ς saepius contra G facere uidemus,' and of this 'frequent' phenomenon five examples are given, one of which is an example where it happens, and four of which are examples where it does not happen; then passages where D and the rest of ς desert G and agree with O are quoted, legitimately, though in stupefying disorder, to prove that ς are not derived from G. Some of these are places where G is wrong and ς are right, on which Mr

Schulze remarks (p. xlvi) 'qua in re ut sane concedendum est facile fuisse librariis uitia illa corrigere, ita mirum est, quamuis sescenties in transcribendis corruptelis scribas summa religione uti uideamus, illas a *cunctis* [Mr Schulze's italics] felicissime esse correctas'. *Cunctis*! why, who ever dreamed of maintaining that each of the scribes made these corrections for himself? Baehrens, as I have related, held that ⛛ were all derived from a single apograph of G, and that all corrections common to all ⛛ were derived from that apograph. But because Messrs Teubner allow Mr Schulze to maul Baehrens' work out of all recognition, he appears to think that he can with equal ease obliterate it from human memory. Then passages are quoted where ⛛ have the reading which by comparing O we infer to have been G's original reading now erased by the corrector g. All these examples of ⛛ agreeing with O against G are of course valid *prima facie* objections to Baehrens' theory. Baehrens' answer was 'talia, si falsa sunt, mero casui adtribuas: sin recta, aut casui aut Italorum ingenio'. This perhaps is not plausible; but on the other hand Mr Schulze has no ground for concluding 'praeter duo illa apographa codicis V, G et O, tertium sumendum est, ex quo deriuati sunt g ⛛, uel potius, cum inter hos quoque D quidem et qui cum eo consentiunt et M insignem obtinere locum uideamus, quartum.' All readings which ⛛ share with O they may have derived from O.

But in order to prove that ⛛ are authorities independent of O and G Mr Schulze now quotes a page and a half of readings from ⛛ which he thinks better than O's and G's. They are all obvious conjectures, except one which is an exploded corruption, one in which he misreports the MSS., one which is probably interpolated from Quintilian, and the following two: '65 16 *Battiadae*] *bactiade* B ⛛ pauci: *actiade* O, *acciade* G. 66 5 *sub Latmia*] *sublamia* B: *sublamina*

O, *sublimia* G ς plerique.' But *bactiade* may be a conjecture, as that was one of the many ways they spelt this name in the 15th century; and *sublamia* may be no more than a corruption of *sublamīa*. Therefore Mr Schulze is mistaken in saying 'nonnulla ea habent expressae sinceritatis signa, ut facere non possimus quin eis fidem habeamus'. Against the view that the good readings in ς are conjectures he has this notable argument: 'nemo quidem credet, eundem correctorem, quem aliis locis hominem indoctum cognouimus, hic illic mira sagacitate optimas correcturas suo ingenio inuenisse.' *Eundem correctorem*! Remember that on p. xlvi it suited him to assume that readings common to all ς must, if conjectures, have been made by each scribe for himself: now, when for instance at 64 120 he finds one MS. and one only giving *praeoptaret*, and giving it merely in the margin, he assumes that this reading must, if a conjecture, have been made by the scribe of the common archetype of all ς.

Then we deal particularly with the two MSS. which Mr Schulze regards as holding an 'insignem locum' among ς. First D, which 'ceteris codicibus hisce praestat locis': the places are 23 in number (and in several of them, since the list is of Mr Schulze's making, other MSS. read just the same as D), some of them obvious conjectures, some bad corruptions, one probably interpolated from Seneca, one in which Mr Schulze contradicts his own apparatus criticus, and these two,—1 2 *arrida*, 25 11 *insuta*, the latter of which is worth something if it is really in the MS.; but these two readings are not found in D by other collators and rest on the testimony of Mr Schulze; and if any one, after hearing what I shall shortly say about M, chooses to accept Mr Schulze's testimony, let him. Then follow passages, proving nothing, where D 'optima tradidit' in company with OG or O or ς; then our old friends the 'priscae uerborum formae' which are no doubt D's most plausible feature; but Mr Schulze has drawn up the list so it contains eleven which are also found in G or O or both: it is true that what he set out to prove was that D is not derived from O or G but from a separate apograph of V; but that was some pages back, so he has forgotten it. Lastly, crown of glory, 'uersum 65 9 paene solus tradidit', *alloquar audiero numquam tua loquentem*. Then are duly enumerated D's faults, its blunders and interpolations, among the latter 68 47 *omnibus et triuiis uulgetur fabula passim*, which would do D even greater credit than *alloquar audiero* but for the mischance that we know it was written by Thomas Seneca.

'Neque minus insignem locum inter ϛ codex M tenere mihi uidetur, qui et ipse magnum numerum bonarum lectionum praebet': this is the Venetus excerpted by Ellis. There follow two pages of these 'bonae lectiones,' many of which of course are bad (one of them is 68 50 where M has the false *alii* and the right reading *Alli* is in O!), while of those which are not bad only one is peculiar to M. True, the reader would never guess this, for Mr Schulze only notes the agreement of other MSS. in about a third of his examples, and leaves you to draw the false inference that in the other two thirds where he does not note their agreement, they do not agree: in another writer this suppression of facts would argue fraud, but no such hypothesis is necessary in the case of Mr Schulze. Not one of the readings quoted has any sign of genuineness. But 'accedunt priscae formae': *e.g. Bithynia, Phrygii, coetus, labyrintheis, cachinni*! Others of these are not peculiar to M but found also in O or G or both or ϛ: the reader has guessed, before I tell him, that Mr Schulze sometimes states this fact and sometimes conceals it. Others contradict his apparatus criticus, as 23 1 *seruos*. *Neptumnus* at 31 3 and *antemne* at 64 234 are

not the readings of M but merely Mr Schulze's interpretation of its readings: it has *neptŭnus* and *antēne*, which
are identical with the *neptunnus* and *antenne* of other MSS.
'Etiam in his lectionibus complures sunt quas non ingenio
scribae deberi manifestum est, ut'—then one of Mr
Schulze's lists, comprising for instance 76 18 *extrema*, which
is undisguisedly a conjectural accommodation of G's and
O's *extremo* to the gender of *morte*; and 25 5 *oscitantes*, which
is in G, so that Mr Schulze need not be at all afraid of our
imputing it 'ingenio scribae'. These readings, he placidly
continues, are confirmed by the fact that most of them are
found in other MSS. (such is the 'insignis locus' occupied
by M), 'whence we may readily infer that the good readings peculiar to M are also derived from V.' On this logic
it is the less necessary to comment, because there are only
two good readings peculiar to M. They are *thuniam* for
thimiam at 31 5 and *hinsidias* for *insidias* at 84 2. And these
two—does my reader flatter himself that he has lost by
this time the power to wonder at anything? I promise to
amaze him now—these two readings, the only two good
readings peculiar to M which Mr Schulze can find, are not
in M at all. They are figments of Mr Schulze's. A facsimile
of M has been issued by Count Nigra and may be seen at
the British Museum: the handwriting is beautifully clear
and the ink is beautifully black: and M gives *thimiam* and
insidias just like any other MS. We see then that Mr Schulze
the collator is in no way inferior to Mr Schulze the critic,
Mr Schulze the metrist, and Mr Schulze the logician.
And with such a collation of such a MS. has Mr Schulze
sullied Baehrens' apparatus criticus from end to end.
Worse: whereas he says that M is derived from V, he
exhibits it throughout as an independent authority, and
you find 'arido VM' at 1 2 and you find 'dabis VM' at
116 8 and you find 'VM' on every page between.

Last comes the question of marginal variants in the archetype. Mr Schulze has taken Baehrens' list of the variants in G, and has mixed up with it all the variants he can find in ꜱ and especially in his precious M; and he, who has himself collated that codex, has done so without discovering what is patent to every one who sets eyes on the facsimile, that nine tenths of its variants are from a later hand. It is clear, he then proceeds to say, that these variants found their way into M and ꜱ not from G but from some other MS.: 'nam cum G octoginta omnino praebeat atque inde ab c. lxvii nullas, M 155 per totum librum Catullianum aequaliter distributas habet.' If you say you have three sons at a school where there are 100 boys, Mr Schulze will ask whether you are the father of the remaining 97, and if you disclaim the honour he will tell you that in that case you cannot really be the father of the three. But he has another argument: 'quodsi omnes ꜱ ex G descripti essent, ponendum est singulares codicum O, M, B, L, aliorum duplices lectiones a scribis horum librorum fictas esse; id quod uel propterea fieri non potest, quod multae earum in textu aliorum extant codicum.' First, observe the ratiocination: because many of the variants in OMBL etc. are found in the text of other codices, therefore the variants in OMBL etc. which are not found in the text of other codices cannot have been invented by the scribes of OMBL etc. Secondly, it is not true that the hypothesis which derives ꜱ from G compels us to suppose that these marginal variants have been invented by the scribes of the MSS. in whose margins they occur: what one naturally supposes is that the variants in the margins of MBL etc. (I do not know what O is doing here, nor does Mr Schulze) have been taken from those other MSS. in whose texts they occur; and this is what Mr Schulze must disprove before he will persuade any one that these variants come from the archetype. But he cannot disprove it: all he can do is to say 'nam si [30 9] in B *inde* al *idem*, in GDL *inde*, in O *idem* legitur, quis dubitet, quin in communi archetypo, codice V, duplex illa scriptura fuerit?' That V had the dittography is possible, since O has one reading and G the other; but B proves nothing unless Mr Schulze can show that it did not get its *inde* from G and its *idem* from O. He however, as if he had proved his point, sails away with 'iam cum M et B neque ex O neque ex G fluxisse certum sit...', and concludes 'itaque ea quoque, quae de uariis lectionibus codicum Catullianorum exposuimus, etiam codices deteriores quos uocant in recensendis poetae carminibus adhibendos esse aperte docent.' Yes, and if I had been in Venice a week before Mr Schulze and had scribbled conjectures of my own in the margin of M while the librarian's back was turned, Mr Schulze, who cannot tell one handwriting from another, would have copied them all into his list, and they would now adorn pp. liv–lix of his prolegomena, and he would be maintaining that M got them from the archetype.

Such are the contents of a book which carries on its title-page the name of Aemilius Baehrens and the monogram of B. G. Teubner.

4. THE MANUSCRIPTS OF PROPERTIUS (1895)[4]

Thus much I have written to adjust Dr Postgate's partial estimate of his new codex L. But * * * he discusses the relations and comparative value of Propertius' MSS. in general. I hoped I had done with this matter for a long time to come; for after all, Propertius' MSS. are not the only things in the world. But apparently, like Nehemiah's builders, one must carry the sword to protect the labours of the trowel. When Baehrens, Leo, Solbisky and I with some thought and pains have got this rather uninteresting garden of the Muses into decent order, here is Dr Postgate hacking at the fence for no discoverable reason unless it is the hope of boasting 'liquidis immisi fontibus apros'. I feel it a hardship, but I suppose it is a duty, to withstand this inroad. Dr Postgate makes his mistakes with a tranquil air of being in the right which is likely enough to satisfy students not possessing my weary familiarity with the subject; so here I put it at their service.

In confusing anew the relations of the MSS. Dr Postgate has two principal aims: to exalt N and to disparage DV. It was easy to foresee that the next writer on Propertius' MSS. would disparage DV: Baehrens had disparaged N, Mr Leo had disparaged O, Mr Solbisky had disparaged AF, I had defended one and all; so to disparage DV was the only way left of being original. Idolatry of N, on the other hand, is nothing new.

'It is in his treatment of the Neapolitanus' says Dr Postgate (p. 63) 'that I find Mr Housman least satisfactory'; and he proceeds to explain why: 'though not the enemy of N, he is its most discriminating friend.' I had said, in my discriminating and unsatisfactory way, that there is no best MS. of Propertius. 'The critics of the future' writes Dr Postgate (p. 71) 'will, unless I am much mistaken, pronounce on the contrary that the Neapolitanus *is* the best MS. of Propertius, best as being the oldest of our witnesses'—but age is no merit. Age is merely a promise of merit, which experience may ratify or annul. The hoary head is a crown of glory, says Solomon, *if it be found in the way of righteousness*. Till we have examined two rival MSS., we presume that the older is the better. When we have examined them, we judge them by their contents. Till we have examined the Ambrosian fragment of Seneca's

tragedies (saec. V) and the codex Etruscus (saec. XI–XII)
we presume that the former has the purer text. When we
have examined them we find that it has not. Just so in
the first decade of Livy: the MS. which is by five or six
centuries the oldest is not the best. The worst texts of
Euripides yet known to man were written in classical
antiquity itself. Useless then to call the Neapolitanus 'best
as being the oldest of our witnesses', unless you can keep
it out of our reach. But Dr Postgate continues 'best again
as the one that presents the greatest amount of truth with
the smallest amount of falsehood'. Then if I set a clerk to
copy out the Teubner text the result will be in Dr Postgate's
opinion a still better MS. than the Neapolitanus, because
it will present a greater amount of truth with a smaller
amount of falsehood. How often must I repeat that the
legitimate glory of a MS. is not correctness but integrity,
and that a MS. which adulterates its text, as N does, forfeits
integrity in direct proportion as it achieves correctness?
Give us our ingredients pure: we will mix the salad: we
will not take it ready made from other cooks if we can
help it. We have the Φ element pure in AF and the Δ
element pure in DV and we can blend them for ourselves
much better than N has blent them. The merits which I
recognise in N are not the age and correctness which Dr
Postgate expects the critics of the future to admire, but
these two: the lesser, that it usefully supplements the pure
but imperfect witness of AF to the tradition of Φ; the
greater, redeeming all its vice, that it contains in its adulterated text a third ingredient which we nowhere possess
in a pure form.

This brings me to speak of a cause to which N owes
more blind worshippers than to either its age or its correctness. Dr Postgate writes (pp. 62 *sq*.) 'a doubt, greater or
less according to circumstances, must rest upon all un-

supported lections in any of the manuscripts AFLDV. There is in fact only one known manuscript of Propertius whose unsupported evidence is to be taken into serious account in any considerable number of passages. I mean of course the Neapolitanus.' That is to say, each of the other MSS. mentioned is so lucky as to possess a near relative which confirms and checks its witness: N has the singular misfortune to possess none. For this whimsical reason do many people call N the best MS. of Propertius. Perhaps the simplest way to dispel the error is the following. Suppose that all extant MSS., with one exception, exhibited a text akin to N's, and that the one exception were our D: those who now on the above grounds call N the best MS. would then be bound by parity of reasoning to call D the best. And, I assure them, they would do so: they would forget all D's faults just as they now forget N's. Yet of course D would not really be a jot better than before. The confusion of thought is here: we do right to rejoice that we possess N rather than a second F or D or V; but we find a wrong vent for that joy when we call N the best MS.: the proper vent is to thank providence. Iron is plentiful in England, so we would rather have the Borrowdale blacklead-mine than one iron-mine more; but we do not therefore call blacklead a better mineral than iron. If however any one is of opinion that the good readings found in N and not in F or D outweigh the good readings found in F or D and not in N, *plus* the excess of F's or D's integrity over N's, then he has a right to call N the best MS. of Propertius. But since I do not see how such a comparison can be carried out with any approach to precision I prefer to state what is roughly true and say that there is no best MS.

5. PALMER'S 'HEROIDES' OF OVID (1899)[5]

* * * Among the critics who have emended Ovid's *Heroides*
since the time of Heinsius the first place belongs to Bentley,
the second to Palmer, and the third to Madvig: van Lennep
and Merkel may dispute for the fourth. The list of Palmer's
emendations which I should call certain or nearly so * * *
is not indeed a long one: it will not compare with what he
effected in Propertius or even in Bacchylides. But in
Propertius, where his achievement equalled Baehrens'
and surpassed Lachmann's, there was much more to be
done; and as for Bacchylides, skimming the first cream
off a new-found author is only child's-play beside gleaning
after Bentley over a stubble where Heinsius has reaped.
There is much to censure in this edition, so I begin with
this tribute: no critic of the century has purified the text so
much, and no critic but Madvig so brilliantly. And since
Palmer's death was not noticed in this *Review* I will say
more. In width and in minuteness of learning, in stability
of judgment, and even in what is now the rarest of the
virtues, precision of thought, he had superiors among his
countrymen and contemporaries: in some of these things
many excelled him, some excelled him far, and Munro
excelled him far in all. But that will not disguise from
posterity and ought not to disguise from us that Palmer
was a man more singularly and eminently gifted by nature
than any English scholar since Badham and than any
English Latinist since Markland.

Then why, both at home and abroad, was he less
esteemed than many of his inferiors? Not only nor perhaps
chiefly because the classical public in England has not
even yet relinquished that false standard of merit which
it adopted after 1825, nor because the great North-German

school of the nineteenth century has begun to decline and has not begun to find out that it is declining, but through his own fault. His talent, like that of Heinsius, resided in felicity of instinct: it did not proceed, like Madvig's, from the perfection of intellectual power. Now the class which includes Heinsius includes also Gilbert Wakefield; and Palmer's rank in the class is nearer to Wakefield than to Heinsius. His inspiration was fitful, and when it failed him he lacked the mental force and rightness which should have filled its place. His was a nimble but not a steady wit: it could ill sustain the labour of severe and continuous thinking; so he habitually shunned that labour. He had no ungovernable passion for knowing the truth about things: he kept a very blind eye for unwelcome facts and a very deaf ear for unwelcome argument, and often mistook a wish for a reason. No one could defend more stubbornly a plain corruption, or advocate more confidently an incredible conjecture, than Palmer when the fancy took him. He had much natural elegance of taste, but it was often nullified by caprice and wilfulness, so that hardly Merkel himself has proposed uncouther emendations. Moreover Palmer was not, even for his own age and country, a learned man. He read too little, and he attended too little to what he read; and with all his genius he remained to the end of his days an amateur. And these defects he crowned with an amazing and calamitous propensity to reckless assertion. * * *

6. TREMENHEERE'S 'CYNTHIA' OF PROPERTIUS
(1900) [6]

'Scholars will pardon an attempt, however bald, to render into English these exquisite love-poems.' Why? Those who have no Latin may pardon such an attempt,

if they like bad verses better than silence; but I do not
know why bald renderings of exquisite love-poems should
be pardoned by those who want no renderings at all. One
who cannot read or understand

> omniaque ingrato largibar munera somno,
>   munera de prono saepe uoluta sinu,

may perhaps pardon the translation

> Ungrateful sleep! Give all I could,
> Roll from your lap my presents would!

But who else? only the personage of whom Heine tells us
'c'est son métier'. Some bald renderings there are which
even scholars will pardon: when Mr Paley sings 'It is
present to me to feel the chill, the very severe chill, of a
hostile public executioner', or Mr Buckley 'They cut off his
ears and nostrils with the sharp brass; but he, injured in
his feelings, went about, enduring that calamity with a
frantic mind', scholars are as grateful as other folk; but
Mr Tremenheere never rejoices the heart like this,
though he does write, 'To eclipse your honoured uncle
strive' and ask 'Is yours the spirit that can brave The hard
bunk and the howling wave?'

The chief merit of his version is its admirable and even
surprising conciseness: he has chosen his metre ill, for our
octosyllabic couplet is not only as much unlike the elegiac
as one couplet can be unlike another, but also affords very
little room; yet nothing essential is omitted, except now
and then the definite article. The phrasing too is often
pointed; but it mostly wants grace and finish and is sometimes ugly: 'When, Gallus, stuttering and agasp, You
languished in the damsel's clasp', 'And, by Hylaeus
bludgeoned well, Lay groaning on the Arcadian fell'.
Where everything else is sacrificed to smartness and 'illa
suis uerbis cogat amare Iouem' is rendered 'She'd coax the

devil to her feet', some will admire; but there is nothing
smart about slang terms like 'cut' and 'wig': they mis-
represent Propertius, who is not a colloquial writer but
literary to a fault, and they are repulsive. Misrepresen-
tation of Propertius is indeed the capital defect of this
performance: good or bad, in movement, in diction, in
spirit, it is unlike the original. I will quote some verses
from the second poem, which is much the best translated:

> Life of my life, why court applause
> In fluttering folds of Coan gauze,
> With Syrian scent on plaits and curls
> And all the gauds of foreign girls?

> * * * * * *

> What beauties e'er with Nature's vied?—
> Wild ivy, meadows gaily pied,
> Lone dells with beauteous berries fraught,
> Clear streams that find their way untaught,
> Bright shores with native gems self-strewn,
> And birds that never learnt a tune!
> 'Twas not their toilets that did win
> Leucippus' daughters each her Twin:
> It was not for a powdered face
> That Pelops came so far to race;
> Nor Idas with Apollo vied
> To bear Marpessa off a bride.

Excellent: the rendering is close and deft, the English is
pure, the phrasing neat, the lines run well; but what was
the Latin? elegiacs by Propertius or hendecasyllables by
Martial? * * *

7. A LINE IN LUCAN (1901)[7]

Mr Heitland says 'a good deal here and elsewhere depends on the value to be assigned to the codex Vossianus primus (V)', and he wishes me to settle this question finally. I have plenty else to do, but perhaps I can enable him to settle it. Nothing here, and not much elsewhere, depends on the value to be assigned to V. That V has some value is admitted: the way to find the amount of that value is to collect the passages, including this iii 276, where its reading is intrinsically more probable than that of the 'Pauline' MSS., to confront these passages with those where its reading is intrinsically less probable, and to see which class is the larger and more important, and by how much. Having thus ascertained the value of V, dismiss it from your mind: never think of it again except in places where the intrinsic probability of V's readings and the 'Pauline' readings is exactly equal. In these places your knowledge of the relative value of V and the 'Paulines' will serve to guide your choice a little better than the method of drawing lots or spinning a coin: not much better; but a little. Such are the precepts of common sense and the practice of my masters Bentley and Madvig. But in Germany they have now adopted another plan, which is very different and much easier. You assume (and if you have luck you may be right in assuming) that one MS. is better than another; and you then proceed to settle, in accordance with this assumption, the intrinsic probability of their readings, endeavouring above all to persuade yourself that the other MS. is as nearly valueless as possible. This is scientific criticism; though liberal shepherds give it the grosser name of putting the cart before the horse. * * *

8. REMARKS ON THE 'CULEX' (1902)[8]

The authors of the *Culex* and *Ciris* and *Aetna* were mediocre poets, and worse, and the gods and men and booksellers whom they affronted by existing allotted them for transcription to worse than mediocre scribes. The *Ciris* was indited by a twaddler, and the *Culex* and *Aetna* by stutterers: but what they stuttered and twaddled was Latin, not double-Dutch; and great part of it is now double-Dutch and Latin no more. * * * Here then, between poets capable of much and copyists capable of anything, is a promising field for the exercise of tact and caution; a prudent editor will be slow to emend the text and slow to defend it, and his page will bristle with the obelus. But alas, it is not for specimens of tact and caution that one resorts to the editors of the *Culex*; it is rather to fill one's bosom with sheaves of improbable corrections and impossible explanations. In particular the editions of Baehrens in 1880 and of Leo in 1891 are patterns of insobriety. * * *

9. OWEN'S PERSIUS AND JUVENAL—A CAVEAT (1904)[9]

I will not take an unfavourable specimen of Mr Owen's reasoning, like the contents of p. 130*b*: I will take an average specimen; and in order to avoid any suspicion of picking and choosing I will take the last sentence of all, which is conveniently brief. 'If O were a mere MS. of the ω class, as Mr Housman contends, it would agree with ω throughout, which it does not.' Now not one known MS. of Juvenal agrees with ω throughout (some MSS., as

Monacensis 408, agree with ω even less than O does, and with P even more than O does). Therefore, on Mr Owen's showing, not one known MS. is a mere MS. of the ω class. Therefore every known MS. is similar in this respect to O. And Mr Owen here believes himself to be arguing that O is a unique MS.

Here I should stop, but for one circumstance, of which I think it right that readers should be warned. Mr Owen has an unfortunate habit of saying things which he believes to be true. He says on p. 126a—

Whereas Mr Housman (*Journal of Philology*, xxi, 101 ff., xxii, 84 ff.) depreciated the Neapolitanus of Propertius and appreciated four late MSS. of the 15th century or thereabouts, and denied the supremacy of the Neapolitanus, which he wished to assign to the 15th century, this house of cards has been lately overthrown, since Mr Montague James has proved (*C.R.* xvii, 462) that the Neapolitanus was written in the 12th century, as Keil long ago maintained, and is consequently by far our earliest MS. of Propertius.

The reader needs to be told that when Mr Owen says I depreciated the Neapolitanus he is attempting to state the fact that I made the most elaborate defence of the Neapolitanus which is anywhere extant; that when he says I appreciated four late MSS. he is attempting to state the fact that I pulled down those four MSS. from the elevation on which they had been placed by Baehrens; and that when he says I wished to assign the Neapolitanus to the fifteenth century he is attempting to state the fact that I declared myself totally indifferent to the question whether the Neapolitanus belonged to the fifteenth century or the twelfth. I think I am right in supposing that an incautious student might be misled by Mr Owen's phraseology. Or let me take—again to avoid any suspicion of picking and choosing—the very first passage which he elects for discussion, Persius i 23, where Madvig *Adv.* ii 128 proposed *articulis* for *auriculis*. Mr Owen here makes two statements, which I contradict. He affirms that this conjecture of Madvig was based on a false reading printed in the text of Priscian by Putsche. I affirm on the contrary that it was based on an examination of all the possible meanings of the MS. reading, on an exposure of the absurdity of all of them, and on an explanation of the requirements of the sense; and that Madvig expressly stated that he had made the conjecture before he knew of any external support for it, false or true: 'veram scripturam iam tum coniectura repertam, cum nondum Iahnii apparatu utebar.' Mr Owen affirms that the traditional text of Pers. i 23 was explained by Nettleship in his edition of Conington. I affirm on the contrary that Nettleship did not even attempt to explain the traditional text, and that what he did was to support a particular interpretation of the two words *cute perditus*, words which Madvig did not propose to alter. The issues are simple, the two books are accessible, and our respective assertions can easily be verified or falsified. If Mr Owen's statements are found true, then you are welcome to believe anything he says about me; even when he attributes to me (p. 126 a) 'an avowed disinclination to allow preponderating authority to one MS. or group of MSS.', which I conjecture to be his closest possible paraphrase of my remark (vol. xvii, p. 390 b) that P is far superior to the whole pack of the other MSS. of Juvenal. But if his statements are found false, then I request as a matter of right that when he makes assertions tending to my discredit he may be disbelieved.

10. ELLIS'S CATULLUS (1905) [10]

Prof. Ellis's place in the annals of Catullian criticism is much like that of Louis XVI in the history of France. He was the unwitting and unwilling author of a revolution. It was he who in the year 1867 brought out from the quiet shade of the Bodleian library that seed of disturbance and innovation, the now famous manuscript O. He then no more suspected what he had found than the son of St Louis guessed what he was doing when he convoked the States General: he allotted the MS. an insignificant place in his stemma codicum and treated it in his recension with almost total indifference. True, he adopted many readings for which O was the sole authority, but it was not on O's authority that he adopted them: they had already been divined by conjecture, and were established in the text of Catullus before 1867. But Baehrens, speciously arguing that a codex containing so many good readings was a good codex and was likely to contain other good readings, announced in 1875 that this was the best MS. of Catullus and moreover that O and G were the sole sources of the text. These plausible opinions have been virtually accepted by the learned world, which agrees that all MSS. but O and G, if not wholly worthless, are practically negligible, and that O, if not the first MS. of Catullus, is the second. * * *

The number of Mr Ellis's conjectures, not including orthographical trifles, is considerably over eighty. But the critics prefer his MS. to his emendations. No editor, I think, has ever accepted more than four of them, and no foreign editor more than two. In my own opinion one of them, 76 11 *te ipse*, is right, a second, 55 11 *reducta pectus*, is probable, two or three more, as 66 55 *pupula*, deserve mention, and a certain number of the rest, though inferior to older corrections, have no positive demerit. But the majority are such as no editor would accept unless he had himself proposed them. * * *

The apparatus criticus is described on the title-page as a *breuis adnotatio*. Brevity and Mr Ellis 'non bene conueniunt nec in una sede morantur', but the notes are perhaps as concise as their authorship allows; they never occupy more than half the page. Whereas most editors, in effect, use two MSS., he uses about two dozen. No, I am wrong: he does not *use* that number; he much oftener quotes them without using them. * * * Sometimes however he does use them, and that is much less innocuous. He mentions in the preface, as a reason for continuing, after the discovery of G and O, to employ the Datanus (one of Lachmann's two chief MSS.), that he highly esteems Lachmann's criticism: 'ego, qui Lachmanni crisin semper habuerim plurimi'. Hereupon I wish to ask three questions. First, where is the connexion? If Lachmann, having no good MSS., used a bad one, is that a reason why Lachmann's disciples, having two good MSS., should use it still? Parisians ate rats in the siege, when they had nothing better to eat: must admirers of Parisian cookery eat rats for ever? My esteem for Lachmann would lead me to act as Lachmann acted not in a dissimilar but in a similar case, in Lucretius, where, having obtained two MSS. as much superior to the rest as G and O are superior to the rest of Catullus' MSS., he based his recension upon these. Secondly, if esteem for Lachmann's criticism checks Mr Ellis from discarding one of Lachmann's two chief MSS., how does it allow him to discard the other, the Santenianus? Last, and most perplexing of all, why does Mr Ellis esteem Lachmann's criticism? His own criticism is pre-Lachmannian and anti-Lachmannian, and his apparatus

is just what an apparatus used to be before Lachmann and
his contemporaries introduced their reforms. Lachmann,
who had none but bad MSS., was content with five of
them: Mr Ellis, who has two good MSS., is not content
with fewer than twenty bad ones into the bargain. And
no MS. is too bad for Mr Ellis to build conjectures on its
corruptions. * * *

Although it is difficult to praise a text containing not
only some twenty of Mr Ellis's conjectures but also no
small number of MS. readings which most scholars think
corrupt,—such Latin as 'leporum disertus puer ac face-
tiarum', such diction and metre as 'Pharsaliam coeunt,
Pharsalia tecta frequentant',—still there are whole poems
and pages which can be read without offence. And although the notes omit some things which deserved record-
ing, they contain all requisite information about the two
important MSS. Considered therefore as a handbook for
students this work may well lay claim to a place in the
world: in all external features it is much superior to its
only competitor, Schwabe's small edition of 1886. Mr
Ellis's fame in Catullian literature continues to repose
entirely upon the ample and unborrowed learning of his
Commentary.

11. BUTLER'S PROPERTIUS (1905)[11]

Paley's Propertius, described by Haupt on its first
appearance as 'liber uulgaris ac futilis', has now long
been antiquated; and Mr Butler has produced a commentary which will generally displace it in the hands of English
students. His book, like Paley's, is a compilation, and
neither in illustration nor exegesis nor criticism does it
add anything of moment to the work of his forerunners.
But the performance has much more life and heartiness

than Paley's, and will prove of much more service to the readers for whom it is designed. Mr Butler has made himself acquainted with a great deal that has been written on Propertius in the last five-and-twenty years, and has taken pains to set out his matter with clearness and precision, qualities which are seen at their best in his treatment of the question whether ii 29 is one poem or two and whether iv 8 19 *sq.* are in their proper place. He brings to his task independence, common sense, intelligent interest, and an open mind: not steady judgment, not sustained attention, and not a sufficient knowledge of Latin in general or of Latin verse in particular or indeed of Propertius himself. * * *

An editor of Propertius is occupied half his time, or ought to be, in settling the text and discussing questions of criticism. Here again Mr Butler shows independence but not stability of judgment, and a brisk but not a penetrating or comprehensive intelligence. His work, as I said before, deserves much more praise than Paley's; and yet, if anyone desired to stock a museum of absurdities, Mr Butler's edition would yield far more treasure to the collector. But Mr Butler must not bear the blame for this; on the contrary, it is a surprise and pleasure to find that the absurdities are so much fewer than might have been anticipated. His defects are due to his environment: he has the misfortune to have been born in an age which is out of touch with Latinity. * * *

I suppose that this is hardly what would be called a favourable review; and I feel the compunction which must often assail a reviewer who is neither incompetent nor partial, when he considers how many books, inferior to the book he is criticising, are elsewhere receiving that vague and conventional laudation which is distributed at large, like the rain of heaven, by reviewers who do not know the truth and consequently cannot tell it. But after all, a portion of the universal shower is doubtless now descending, or will soon descend, upon Mr Butler himself; and indeed, unless some unusual accident has happened, he must long ere this have received the punctual praises of the *Scotsman*.

12. LVCILIANA (1907)[12]

In 1871 it might well have been said that no Latin author was in worse need of a critical recension than Lucilius, and again in 1904 that none was in worse need of an exegetical commentary. The one want was supplied in 1872 by the edition of Lucian Mueller, and now Mr Friedrich Marx, by the publication of his second volume in 1905, has supplied the other. Both works deserve praise, both deserve thanks, and both deserve more thanks than praise; for while gratitude is earned simply by the element of good which a book presents to us, admiration must depend on the greater or less predominance of the good element over the bad.

The principal service rendered by Mueller's edition was that it provided scholars for the first time with precise and adequate information about the best available MSS. of Nonius and of the other authors by whom Lucilius' fragments have been rescued. For the correction of those fragments it did something, but considerably less. Lucian Mueller, though a consummate metrist, a sound grammarian, and a literary man, was a somewhat superficial critic of no remarkable ingenuity, who emended Lucilius, like the other poets whom he edited, with much more promptitude than skill. The chief value possessed by the commentary of Mr Marx resides in its large collection of relevant facts and its provision of the necessary material on which to found true judgments or probable opinions. To the actual interpretation of the author it also makes a welcome contribution; but Mr Marx's readiness to explain is considerably greater than his faculty for explaining.

The truth is that the difficulties of the text of Lucilius are for the most part inexplicable and its corruptions for the most part irremediable. What more than anything else enables the critic and commentator of an ancient author to correct mistakes and to elucidate obscurities is their context; and a fragment has no context. An editor of Lucilius or Ennius or Nonius or the *Reliquiae scaenicae*, unless he is grievously self-deluded, must know that the greater number of his corrections, and of his explanations also, are false. There is a simple test, if he cares to use it. The bulk of Lucilius' fragments is preserved to us by Nonius only: take Nonius' citations of an author whose works survive, try to explain or emend them, and then compare your efforts with the author's text. * * *

It is therefore no praise of an editor of Lucilius to say that he is conservative, and it is false to say that any editor of Lucilius is cautious. Cautious men do not edit Lucilius; they leave him to be edited by bold and devoted men, whose heroism they admire with that mixture of pity and self-congratulation which a Roman may be supposed to have felt as he saw Curtius descend into the gulf, or an Israelite as he watched the departure of the scapegoat into the wilderness.

Mr Marx's work, considered merely as an illustrative commentary, deserves almost the highest praise; his reading is so wide and his memory so retentive that hardly any Latin poet is now better provided than Lucilius with matter subsidiary to his interpretation. Very seldom have I noticed the omission of a relevant example. * * * The only general fault to be found with his notes is that they contain superfluous matter and are diffusely and sometimes negligently written.

Even when we pass from the illustration of the text to the much higher and harder task of its interpretation there is in Mr Marx's commentary a good deal to admire. He is neither, like some learned commentators, incapable of thought, nor, like others, averse to it; he goes patiently and circumspectly to work, approaches a question from more sides than one, and weighs or tries to weigh the probability of alternative solutions. To say that he then pronounces judgment in accordance with the evidence would be to say too much; for sometimes, after stating the case fairly enough, he will snap off the discussion with an 'ego arbitror' which has no reason to support it. But still, in a certain number, though not a large number, of passages, he has succeeded in clearing up what his predecessors had left dark; and in others he has offered interpretations which to say the least are plausible and attractive and worthy of provisional acceptance. * * *

When we come to conjectural emendation proper, here too Mr Marx has accomplished something, though nothing great. * * * But of his conjectures in general the best thing to be said is that they are somewhat less numerous than the conjectures of Mueller or Baehrens. Very few deserve any better name than tolerable, most of them are either tame or clumsy, and they are sometimes violent, sometimes causeless, and frequently absurd. * * *

And now we are come to the outskirts of that perilous region in which an editor of Lucilius encounters his severest trial. The question is for ever arising whether the tradition of the MSS. is true or false; and, because the relics of Lucilius are fragmentary, it is often very hard to answer. An editor, to acquit himself here with credit, requires three things: ample knowledge, sure judgment, and strict impartiality. Mr Marx's impartiality and judgment, it is already plain, leave something to be desired; and so also does his knowledge.

That a scholar should undertake to edit a poet without first acquiring a due familiarity with metre is no doubt improper, but it has now so often happened that it causes little indignation or surprise. The present age, moreover, is not an age of metrists. * * * Mr Marx indeed has more tact than some of his contemporaries, and does not propose to variegate dactylic poetry with Mr Stowasser's comic scansions. * * * But his knowledge of metre is not adequate to his task. * * *

And now, in the perilous field I spoke of, in those many places where the question arises whether the text is right or wrong, how is this editor to answer it? He cannot; he lacks the requisite knowledge. He misapprehends what Romans have said, and he misconceives the Roman way of saying things: that he should decide whether Lucilius could and would have written what the MSS. impute to him is therefore impossible, and that he should offer to decide it is presumptuous. And then, to make matters worse, in the midst of his difficulties and disabilities, he is assailed by temptation.

In Germany at the present moment, as everyone knows, an editor who wishes to be praised (unless, like one or two influential persons, he has a troop of retainers who will applaud whatever he does) must be a conservative editor; that is to say, he must defend the MS. tradition not only where it appears to be right but also where it appears to be wrong. Some credit, it is true, may be drawn from the mere pronunciation of shibboleths; and Mr Marx, by speaking ill of Mueller and Baehrens and by calling Mr Buecheler 'criticorum facile princeps', has secured at the outset a favourable hearing from a large audience in more lands than one. But this lip-service, though good so far as it goes, is not sufficient: an editor is expected to prove the sanity of his judgment and the orthodoxy of his opinions by defending at least a dozen MS. readings which no former editor has thought defensible; and to this requirement Mr Marx, for want of the knowledge which might have let and hindered him, is quite ready to accede. It is true, as we have seen already, that he does not conserve the text very rigorously against his own conjectures; but he is willing enough to practise the conservative method in its easiest, commonest, and most agreeable form, by preferring the tradition of the MSS. to the conjectures of other people. * * *

A good emendation, in these days, means an emendation which has been proposed by a *persona grata*; and Mr Marx feels sure that most of his readers will regard this conjecture as sufficiently condemned by its authorship. Baehrens has attained the proud position, which he is far indeed from having deserved, of being as much hated by the Germans as Scaliger is hated by the French or Bentley by the English.

But the most arresting feature in Mr Marx's edition is neither the resolution with which he defends Lucilius' fragments against other folk's alterations, nor the faint-heartedness with which he surrenders them to his own, but the facility, the confidence, and the boundless knowledge with which he explains their relation to one another and to their lost and unforthcoming context. For interpreting those words and sentences which we possess in black and white, his aptitude, as we have already seen, is not remarkable; but in the invisible world he is quite at home. Apion, unless he was the liar Josephus thought him, called up the spirit of Homer from the dead, and ascertained from his own melodious lips the true city and parentage of that widely born and many-fathered man. But the information thus elicited he kept secret in the deep of his heart, and the world was none the wiser. Mr Marx, like Apion, is an adept in the black art, but he is not, like Apion, a dog in the manger. He is brimful of knowledge which he can only have acquired by necromancy, and he puts it all at our disposal. * * * Mr Marx should write a novel. Nay, he may almost be said to have written one; for his notes on book iii (Lucilius' journey to Sicily) are not so much a commentary on the surviving fragments as an original narrative of travel and adventure.

'Audacia' is the chief crime which Mr Marx (i, p. cxv) imputes to Mueller; to Mueller, who on p. xliii of his preface has these sober observations, 'fragmentis explicandis uel copulandis nihil facilius esse, si uulgi plausum spectes, neque difficilius quidquam, si peritorum, pridem sanxit auctoritas prudentium'. But when Mr Marx and his school talk about 'audacia' they do not mean audacity, they mean alteration of the text; and they would be surprised to hear that the fabrication of imaginary contexts has any audacity about it. Just as murder is murder no longer if perpetrated by white men on black men or by patriots on kings; just as immorality exists in the relations of the sexes and nowhere else throughout the whole field of human conduct; so a conjecture is audacious when it is based on the letters preserved in a MS., and ceases to be audacious, ceases even to be called a conjecture, when, like these conjectural supplements of Mr Marx's, it is based on nothing at all. No editor of these fragments, neither Mueller nor Baehrens, has been so rash and venturesome as Mr Marx; none has such cause to wish that the earth may lie heavy on Herculaneum and that no roll of Lucilius may ever emerge into the light of day.

13. THE CAMBRIDGE HISTORY OF ENGLISH
LITERATURE, VOL XI: 'THE PERIOD OF THE
FRENCH REVOLUTION' (1915)[13]

It is to be supposed that when the people of England demanded, as apparently they did, a new history of its literature, their desire was not so much for a history which should issue from the Cambridge Press as for a better account of the matter than they had already. In this eleventh volume they will find 100 pages of bibliography, presumably full and accurate; a table of principal dates which would be nearer perfection if it recorded Gray's death instead of Hogarth's, and Macaulay's birth instead of Balzac's or Charles Darwin's; and chapters written with knowledge and sobriety on Burke, Cowper, Crabbe, Blake, Burns, Wordsworth, Coleridge, the lesser poets and lesser novelists of the period, the utilitarian philosophers, the political writers, the drama, prosody, and blue-stockings of the Georgian age, the production and distribution of books from 1625 onward, and the writing of books for children down to 1889. But yet one could wish that this history of English literature were rather more literary and rather more historical.

History need not adhere to chronology, and such anachronisms as the inclusion of Peacock in this volume and the postponement of Scott till the next are shifts of expediency which have no historical importance. But the order of date should be kept where nothing is gained by inverting it. Nothing is gained, nay much is lost, by an inversion which places Wordsworth on p. 93, Crabbe on p. 140, and Blake and Burns on still later pages; for this is an inversion not simply of chronological but of historical sequence. Historically considered, Wordsworth is the pivot of the epoch, and indeed the chief figure in English poetry after Chaucer, if redemption ranks next to creation. No poet later born, not even Campbell, entirely escaped his influence; and 1798 is in the literature of England what 1789 is in the polity of France. But Burns was dead when the *Lyrical Ballads* were published, and Crabbe might have been dead too for all the good or harm they did him. Blake, it may be said, belongs to no age, and is a star that might have shot from heaven at any hour of the night; but, appearing when he did, he was the morning star, the harbinger of Wordsworth, and that is his place, not indeed in literature, but in its history. Again, it is not an historical arrangement which entrusts the treatment of Wordsworth and Coleridge to different hands: the achievements of Castor and Pollux should not be recounted separately, but in one article, *Dioscuri*.

These are faults of design and disposition: the literary shortcomings of the work are diffused, though unequally, among the contributors. The contributors are twelve, and their number does not include the two critics whom one would most have hoped and expected to find here, Mr Andrew Bradley and Sir Walter Raleigh. Expectation, if not hope, is gratified by the presence of Professor Saintsbury, whose abundant knowledge, immense gusto, and general soundness of judgment make him readable even when he is discussing Southey and Peacock for the third or fourth time, airing prejudices neither new nor relevant, and using the barbarous language to which we are now inured. *Gryll Grange* 'has a wonderful absence of glaring Rip-van-Winkleism'. Traces of Coleridge's hand in a book of Southey's are 'Estesian proofs'. If this adjective sends any readers on a wild-goose chase, first to the New English Dictionary and then to the ducal annals of Modena and Ferrara, Mr Saintsbury will feel that it has not been coined in vain; and a reviewer who guided the wanderers to Coleridge's poem beginning *A bird, who for his other sins*, would be regarded by Mr Saintsbury as a spoil-sport. The best writers among the contributors write upon subjects of no great literary moment. The most lucid and graceful chapter is Dr Sorley's on Bentham and the Utilitarians; next comes Mr Routh's on the Georgian drama. But not one of the chapters dealing with the principal figures gives any lively or continuous pleasure by its style or diction, and the account of the greatest prose-writer is written in the worst prose. The estimate conveyed is sound, the reflexions just—'Burke's political aphorisms are so pregnant that they distend the mind with the same sense of fulness with which Shakespeare's lines affect the student of the passions and movements of the human heart'—and the expression sometimes pointed—'the speech *On Conciliation*...remains some compensation to English literature for the dismemberment of the British empire'; but progress through its clumsy and invertebrate sentences is like plodding over a ploughed field of clay. It opens thus:

Edmund Burke, the greatest of English orators, if we measure greatness not by immediate effect alone but by the durability and the diffusive power of that effect, and one of the profoundest, most suggestive and most illuminating of political thinkers, if we may not call a philosopher one who did not elaborate any system and who refrained on principle from the discussion of purely theoretical issues, was an Irishman...;

and there is worse to follow.

It might be contended that, fleeing from one abstraction, he drew near to another, and consecrated prescription, inherited right, when judged and condemned by that expediency which is the sanction of prescription:

the reader discovers in process of time that *consecrated* is one part of speech and *inherited* another.

Whatever be now our judgment on the questions of a bygone age with which he was concerned, the importance of the principles to which his mind always gravitated, his preoccupation at every juncture with the fundamental issues of wise government, and the splendour of the eloquence in which he set forth these principles, an eloquence in which the wisdom of his thought and the felicity of his language and imagery seem inseparable from one another, an eloquence that is wisdom (not 'seeming wisdom' as Hobbes defined eloquence), have made his speeches and pamphlets a source of perennial freshness and interest:

importance, *preoccupation*, and *splendour* are not, like *questions*, governed by the preposition *on*, but are subjects of the verb *have made*, which the reader finds waiting for him on the further side of the anaphora and the parenthesis: then he must start again at the other end of the alligator and retrace the whole length of its dislocated spine. In the last sentence of the chapter the writer has tried to say that Johnson differed from Burke in party politics: what he has succeeded in saying is that Johnson, Goldsmith, and Reynolds differed from one another.

In this chapter it is the form which is not literary: in others it is the attitude and the writers' conception of their subject. Every figure of the first order in this volume, excepting Burke, is a poet. Now the centre of interest in a poet is his poetry: not his themes, his doctrines, his opinions, his life or conduct, but the poetical quality of the works he has bequeathed to us. Therefore a chapter on Wordsworth ought not to begin like this:

Wordsworth's surprise and resentment would surely have been provoked had he been told that, at half a century's distance and from an European point of view, his work would seem, on the whole, though with several omissions and additions, to be a continuation of the movement initiated by Rousseau. It is, nevertheless, certain that it might be described as an English variety of Rousseauism, revised and corrected, in some parts, by the opposite influence of Edmund Burke.

The European view of a poet is not of much importance unless the poet writes in Esperanto. Wordsworth wrote in English; from a European point of view the three great English poets are Shakespeare, Byron, and the late Mr Wilde; and it is no cause for surprise or resentment that Wordsworth, from the same point of view, should seem on the whole to be a continuator of a French or Genevan prose-writer. Then we hear of his 'fundamental tenets', his 'faith in the goodness of nature as well as in the excellence of the child', his 'ideas on education', his 'diffidence in respect of the merely intellectual processes of the mind', his 'trust in the good that may accrue to man from the cultivation of his senses and feelings'. Poetry is no matter of fundamental tenets; faith in the goodness of nature is no more poetical than faith in Jupiter and Juno; and that quality in Wordsworth which alone preserves from oblivion his faith and tenets is one which he did not derive from Burke or Rousseau and could not derive from any writer of prose. There are poets whose poetry is not their chief title to fame: Chaucer and Burns, if all poetical quality were taken away from them, would keep more than they lost and would still be great men of letters, because they are rich in merits which are not poetical. Wordsworth is a much greater poet than either; but if the poetical element were withdrawn from his works he would be only a mediocre man of letters. And the mediocre man of letters is the main theme of this chapter on Wordsworth. There is talk of his moral doctrine, his realism, his attitude to nature, none of them poetical in essence; there is much talk of his optimism, which is downright unpoetical: of his poetry there is less talk, and the fact seems to be that the writer does not feel Wordsworth's poetry. True, he selects for especial praise the two very best and most characteristic stanzas. *Will no one tell me what she sings*, and

No motion has she now, no force; but these have so often been
selected for praise already that he would have proved his
competency better by choosing some other stanzas of the
same inimitable virtue, *My eyes are dim with childish tears*,
or *And I can listen to thee yet*. His favourite piece, which
he mentions four times over, is *The Ruined Cottage*, em-
bodied in the first book of *The Excursion*, 'a perfect poem,
such as Wordsworth never surpassed', 'he never outdid
that pastoral and, indeed, only once or twice again reached
such perfection'. Now *The Ruined Cottage* is a simple and
pathetic story of misfortune, told in pure English and good
verse; but the heavenly alchemy is absent. 'The tale,' says
the critic, 'is most distressing and desolate', and he
innocently adds 'Wordsworth's usual optimism is not to
be found in it'. For that relief much thanks; but if *The
Ruined Cottage* were 'a perfect poem', it would be exalting
and not distressing. The fourteenth chapter of Job is not
distressing, nor the *Antigone*, nor even *King Lear*. And at
such a sentence as 'these instances tend to prove that his
poetry is not identical with his habitual teaching, that it
sometimes revolts against it, that it may here and there
go beyond it', one asks oneself what the writer can possibly
mean by poetry. How can any poetry be identical with
any teaching? It would not however be fair to quit this
chapter without acknowledging that it contains true
things well said: 'his undisputed sovereignty (as a poet of
nature)...lies in his extraordinary faculty of giving
utterance to some of the most elementary and at the same
time obscure sensations of man confronted by natural
phenomena'; 'if he thought like others, he always thought
by himself. He gives us the impression that, had he lived
alone on a bookless earth, he would have reached the
same conclusions.'

The volume conveys plenty of information, and especially

8   C H

in the chapters on the Georgian drama and the production
and distribution of books it collects information which is
not collected elsewhere. Its estimates of the principal
authors are generally the accepted estimates, and accepted
estimates of literature more than a hundred years old are
likely to be somewhere near the truth. What it lacks is
quality. If one tries to picture a reader cherishing this
volume, the image does not come at call.

14. A GEORGIAN HISTORY OF VICTORIAN LITERATURE (THE CAMBRIDGE HISTORY OF ENGLISH LITERATURE, VOLS. XIII AND XIV) (1917) [14]

These two volumes complete the Cambridge history of
English literature and embrace that period which is
commonly and almost accurately entitled the Victorian
age. The names included range from Carlyle, who was
born before Keats and began to write under George IV,
to Meredith and Swinburne, who lived on, and, alas,
wrote on, through most of King Edward's reign; but all
the chief names are those of men who did their chief work
between 1837 and 1901. Newman is not here, but has
probably found an earlier place in some chapter sacred to
religion: the living also are excluded, and the youngest
writer of note who receives notice is Francis Thompson,
born in 1859.

The Victorian age of literature has been disparaged, as
the manner is, by 'ces enfants drus et forts d'un bon lait
qu'ils ont sucé, qui battent leur nourrice', and, like most
other ages, it was assiduously depreciated by some of its
own chief ornaments. 'It is odd that the last 25 years',
wrote Macaulay in 1850, 'should have produced hardly a

volume that will be remembered in 1900'; and in 1855 'the general sterility, the miserably enervated state of literature' was still prevailing. But it is now safe to say that the Queen's reign was a great age of English letters, the more remarkable because it followed almost without pause upon a greater. France in the same years produced perhaps as good a crop as England, but that field had lain fallow for a whole generation. One great age of literature exhausted Germany; one age of literature less than great has exhausted America; but never since the defeat of the Armada has great literature ceased to flourish and renew itself in the island home of inefficiency.

Whether the time has yet come to weigh one Victorian author against another, or one work against another of the same author's, is not so sure.

The tuneful quartos of Southey are already little better than lumber:— and the rich melodies of Keats and Shelley,—and the fantastical emphasis of Wordsworth,—and the plebeian pathos of Crabbe, are melting fast from the field of our vision. The novels of Scott have put out his poetry. Even the splendid strains of Moore are fading into distance and dimness, except where they have been married to immortal music; and the blazing star of Byron himself is receding from its place of pride.... The two who have the longest withstood this rapid withering of the laurel, and with the least marks of decay on their branches, are Rogers and Campbell.

So wrote the first professional critic of his time when the greatest age of English literature had just reached its close; and this judgment he reprinted in 1843, and again in 1846, more than twenty years from the end of that age and nearly fifty from its beginning. But there is reason to hope that we can now judge Victorian writers less perversely than Jeffrey is seen to have judged their predecessors. Jeffrey was a little younger than Wordsworth, and had formed his taste before the year 1798, when the Lord created a new thing in the earth. All the critics who contribute to these volumes were bred in the Victorian tradition, and most of them were born much later than the authors committed to them for criticism. The Victorian age, moreover, introduced no great and disconcerting change; it did but develop and modify existing tendencies, with some progress and some relapse. The pause after 1824 was nothing but a momentary dearth of great writers, no prelude to any tide of revolution rolling under the breath of a Wordsworth or carrying a Dryden on its crest. The more salient novelties of Victorian literature were not durable and have now lost their vogue; except that for some few years a novelist or two will still sport the suit of buckram which Meredith ordered at his tailor's to disguise the failure of his genius. No author of the time has exercised the permanent influence of Keats or Scott. Browning had no following, Tennyson had no following that mattered, and Carlyle's endeavour to naturalise in England the style of Jean Paul Richter is a long way further from accomplishment than his wish to substitute a Hindenburg for the British constitution. In the sixties it seemed indeed as if there had arisen a band of writers to launch poetry on a new career; but time showed that they were cruising in a backwater, not finding a channel for the main stream, and in twenty years all heart had gone out of the enterprise. The fashions of that interlude are already so antique that Mr Gilbert Murray can adopt them for his rendering of Euripides; and there they now receive academic approbation, which is the second death.

It is probable that these volumes reflect with due fidelity the current estimate of Victorian authors and their works. If posterity is surprised to find ten pages about William Morris and less than two about Coventry Patmore, it will also be instructed; for this scale unquestionably corresponds to the prevalent opinion of 1916 and even 1917. But a list of 'Lesser Poets' comprising Dobell and Francis Thompson as well as Patmore may provoke some wonder even now, if it is borne in mind that 'lesser' means lesser than Clough, James Thomson, and O'Shaughnessy. That Carlyle should have twenty-two pages to Macaulay's eight reflects perhaps rather the estimate of three years since, Carlyle's repute being now a trifle damaged by our temporal relations with his spiritual home. And posterity will probably be wrong if it infers that most of us thought two pages enough for Stevenson in a work where George Gissing has more than seven, or a page and a quarter enough for Pater, a true man of letters though not a great one, in a work where Froude, who was base metal all through, has three and a half.

The criticism of the twenty-four contributors is sober and for the most part competent, but not every subject is judiciously allotted. For example, a writer who is qualified to treat of Thackeray may yet be ill sorted with 'The Rossettis, William Morris, Swinburne and others'. The chapter on Tennyson, though rather clumsily written, is perhaps the best, and does justice alike to the greatness and the pettiness of its theme. The worst chapter, without any perhaps, is that on Anglo-Irish literature, in which the thinking is as flaccid as the writing.

But it now seems fairly certain, in the opinion of Windisch and other Celtic scholars, including Quiggin, that some of the Welsh rhapsodists apparently served a kind of apprenticeship with their Irish brethren.

On the same page it is suggested that Shakespeare may have got what Matthew Arnold calls his note of Celtic magic 'at second hand, through Edmund Spenser, or his friend Dowland the lutenist, who, if not an Irishman, had

an Irish association'. Let us all seek the society of Mr
A. P. Graves and then perhaps we too shall write things
like *daffodils That come before the swallow dares, and take The
winds of March with beauty*; though it is true that Mr Graves
himself, like Dowland and Spenser, does not.

In an interesting chapter on 'changes in the language
since Shakespeare's time' it is said that the fear of degen-
eration expressed by Johnson in the preface to his dictionary has not yet been justified. But it has; and these
volumes are one small part of the justification. 'In prose,'
wrote Coleridge a hundred years ago, 'I doubt whether
it be even possible to preserve our style wholly unalloyed
by the vicious phraseology which meets us everywhere.
Our chains rattle, even while we are complaining of them.'
And the English language, since Coleridge wrote, has
continued to deteriorate in fibre. Is there, can there be,
such a word as *purposive*? There is: it was invented by a
surgeon in 1855; and instead of being kept on the top
shelf of an anatomical museum it is exhibited in both
these volumes. And the decline is not only in our language
but in our skill to use it. Before the middle of the eighteenth
century the writing of good English had ceased to come
by nature, but it was widely and successfully practised as
an art. The common stock of words was already both
impoverished and contaminated, but there was a high
and strict tradition of comeliness in style. This is extinct,
and our bricklaying is no better than our bricks. It is now
possible, nay usual, to spend a lifetime in the study of
literature without ever learning the knack of it, and no
reader opening this book will even expect to find the
dyer's hand subdued to what it works in. Two hundred
years ago John Dennis was reckoned a dunce; but no
chapter here can compare with his *Remarks upon Cato* for
race and flavour of diction or for spring and terseness of

style. Soame Jenyns was an old woman and his vocabulary was as trite as could be; and yet, because he wrote in the eighteenth century, he put his poor words and thoughts into shipshape sentences. But written English is now inert and inorganic: not stem and leaf and flower, not even trim and well-joined masonry, but a daub of untempered mortar. The following extracts, it is fair to say, are not typical examples of the work; but that they should make their appearance in a history of literature is noteworthy and significant.

There was, however, never so much difference in his case between the public and, at first, a few, but, latterly, nearly all, critics as occurred in the case of Lewis Morris, who, also, was later knighted.

The somewhat epicene touch (acknowledged long after it had been recognised by some under the for a long time well-kept pseudonym Fiona Macleod) by William Sharp can receive no extended notice here.

The editor of the nearly finished (fourth) volume left behind him by Gairdner of his *Lollardy and the Reformation* considers that, in writing the section on *The History of the English Church*, of which Gairdner's later work was an unfinished enlargement, he (though already at an advanced age) believed himself to be fulfilling a duty; and he, certainly, had the cause of truth at heart.

Since, in 1786, he had (though matters of finance were never much to his taste) in an admired maiden speech attacked Pitt's commercial treatises, he never faltered, either in the days of the eclipse of the whig party, or in those of catholic emancipation (in which he delivered a speech which Stanley (Derby) said he would rather have made than four of Brougham's) and of reform.

Nor does it mend matters to stick in sprigs of ornament.

All...pay unconstrained honour to Swinburne's celebration of his ideals of liberty and justice, clothed in music which is borne upon the wings of the wind and wails and rejoices, now loud with delight in its beauty and strength and now threatening or plaintive in its anger or sadness, like the voice of the sea.

As rhetoric this is puerile, as criticism it is null. It is like what the *Daily Chronicle* said when Matthew Arnold died;

and that is worth communicating to those who do not
know it already.

His music mounted upward with bright thoughts, as the skylark
shakes dewdrops from its wing as it carols at 'Heaven's Gate,' or,
like a mountain brooklet carrying many a wild flower on its wavelets,
his melody flowed cheerily on. Sometimes too his music rises like
that of the mysterious ocean casting up pearls as it rolls.

The value of the work as a repertory of information
is not affected by lumpish writing nor even by disputable
judgments, and it is certainly an ample and probably a
trustworthy collection of facts. There is however one
department of which so much cannot be said. Upon what
principle, and from what materials, the bibliography has
been compiled, is far from clear; but it does not seem that
either the *Dictionary of National Biography* or the general
catalogue of the University Library has been consulted.
Completeness was not to be expected or even desired in
a book of this compass; but the information supplied is
in many cases neither adequate nor accurate, and even
the memory of a reader conversant with the period
will enable him to correct mistakes and repair omissions.
Here are three entries in the 'Table of Principal Dates',
vol. xiii, p. 576. '1863 Lear's *Book of Nonsense*': its date
was 1846. '1877 Palgrave's *Golden Treasury*': its date was
1861. '1908 Thompson's *The Hound of Heaven*': its date
was 1893, and Thompson died in 1907.

15. BYWATER'S 'FOUR CENTURIES OF GREEK LEARNING IN ENGLAND' (1920)[15]

This lecture, which Bywater probably thought too slight
for publication, has been found among his notebooks
and is issued from the press of his University. It is the
business-like performance of a good scholar who did not

aspire to be an indifferent man of letters; and readers who wish to hear about the Greek spirit may leave it alone.

The greatest part of it is occupied with matter of the least importance. The renascence of learning in England is history in which Bywater was at home, and he collects a large number of details which I presume to be accurate and which have some interest of a purely antiquarian sort. But those were the years when we were learning Greek and were not yet in case to teach it: our contribution to the European fund begins with the seventeenth century. In Bywater's account of this period there is nothing which I can gainsay of my own knowledge; though I should have thought that Pearson, of whom Bentley said that the very dust of his writings was gold, and Porson that he would have equalled even Bentley as a critic in Greek if he had not muddled his brains with divinity, deserved more prominence than is given him. The two pages on Bentley himself are excellent; and laymen who wonder at the fame of this tasteless and arbitrary pedant, and the reverence paid him by every competent judge, will hardly find elsewhere in so small a compass so clear a definition of his unique originality and greatness.

But in Bywater's sketch of Greek scholarship after Bentley there are places where I find his judgment or his knowledge defective. He says with truth that Bentley's chief successors, excepting Taylor and in some measure Toup and Tyrwhitt, were mostly occupied, like Bentley himself, with the poets; and I surmise that for this very reason they were not familiar to Bywater.

The school of Bentley, if the expression may be hazarded, Markland, Dawes, Musgrave, Warton, and the rest, allowed itself to be absorbed in the study of the Greek poets. If I were asked who was the strong man and chief figure in this company, I should say with little hesitation, Richard Dawes.

Warton makes a strange appearance here, though far be it from me to blame Bywater or anyone else for ignorance of his large and empty Theocritus; and I should have liked to watch Bentley from a safe distance in Elysium when he heard the expression hazarded that Warton was one of his school. Although the pre-eminence assigned to Dawes is disputable, I will not dispute it, and I grudge him no praise; but *strong* is not the right word to praise him with. His special virtue was a preternatural alertness and insight in the two fields of metre and grammar, the more extraordinary because his mere learning was not profound. The *strong* man of the company was Markland, devoid of these peculiar qualities, but superior in range and vigour and general activity of mind. It is probable that Englishmen are right in counting Porson the second of English scholars, but many judges on the Continent would give that rank to Markland. He is the only one except Bentley who has been highly and equally eminent in Greek and Latin; and I believe that Bentley did him the honour, extravagant I admit, to be jealous of him.

Porson...is...a model of caution and patience, not an impetuous genius like Bentley or Dawes.

Certainly Porson had less genius and less impetuosity than Bentley, but he had as much genius as Dawes, and Dawes had not much more impetuosity than Porson: those who think he had are misled by the effervescence of his style, and its unlikeness to Porson's constraint. There may have been impetuosity, or at least some lack of caution, in Dawes's canon about ὅπως μή with the 1st aor. subj. active and middle and his alteration of Ar. *Ach.* 633 and *Pac.* 918, but so there was in Porson's pronouncement on the form of the 2nd pers. sing. pres. indic. passive and his destruction of the metre of Eur. *Med.* 629.

The Porsonian school, Blomfield, Monk, and Elmsley, if I may include him among them, continued Porson's work on the dramatists, though with little of Porson's freshness or felicity of touch.

This is true of Monk, if not of Blomfield, but of Elmsley it is false and unjust. Elmsley no doubt was distinctly inferior to Porson as an emendator, though still a good one, but he was not much inferior as an observer and discoverer in grammar and metre, and his writing has a candour and a pleasant irony which are graces not easily to be matched. See how Nauck and Wilamowitz speak of him, or hear the words of his great antagonist Hermann:

Est enim P. Elmsleius, si quis alius, uir natus augendae accuratiori Graecae linguae cognitioni, ut cuius eximia ac plane singularis in peruestigandis rebus grammaticis diligentia regatur praeclaro ingenio, mente ab auctoritatibus libera, animo ueri amantissimo, neque aut superbia aut gloriae studio aut obtrectandi cupiditate praepedito. his ille uirtutibus id est consecutus, ut, cum doctrina eius maximi facienda sit, non minus ipse sit amandus atque uenerandus.

And this one slighting mention is all that the Regius Professor of Greek at Oxford could spare for the most famous scholar that Oxford ever produced. He continues 'if the mantle of the master descended on anyone, it was rather on Dobree'. It is very hard to decide between the merits of Dobree and Elmsley: I should say that the mantle came in two and half of it fell on each; Dobree was the shrewder emendator and Elmsley the subtler grammarian.

The statement on p. 15 that 'Porson edited Photius' is not strictly true, and on p. 18 the death of Badham is post-dated by five years.

16. SIMPSON'S 'LOUIS NAPOLEON AND THE RECOVERY OF FRANCE' (1923)[16]

Fourteen years ago there was published by a country curate a study of the third Napoleon's ascent from the cradle to the Presidency of the Republic which placed its author among the best living historians. *The rise of Louis Napoleon* is now followed by *Louis Napoleon and the recovery of France*, continuing the story from 1848 to 1856 and confirming Mr Simpson's reputation. The same virtues reappear: originality, integrity, sobriety, research, a sprightly and engaging style, a strong turn for epigram, and a great deal of pleasant malice expended upon such objects as most invite it and deserve it—historians, republicans, the British nation, and the human race. The writing is not so easy and equable as in the earlier volume, and the epigrams, though more brilliant and abundant, are not always so naturally or artfully introduced as epigrams should be; but the style has yet so much grace and vigour that one wishes the diction were purer than it is. It would be pedantry in a history of 1851 to eschew *coup d'état*; but who can imagine *sotto voce* or πάρεργον on a page of Macaulay? The slang with which Mr Simpson now and then defiles his pen is probably slang which he heard in his cradle and believed in his innocence to be English: 'a settlement *of sorts*' for example on p. 362, which does not mean what Shakespeare would suppose, but only that Mr Simpson has no high opinion of the settlement. Here too, as everywhere, are the daisies and dandelions of contemporary metaphor. Till I read p. 241 I did not know that a storm could have an aftermath nor that an aftermath could reach a throne; but I have since found the same blend of meteorology and agriculture in a novel of Mr Hugh Walpole's—though the aftermath is there a 'faint' one and so no throne is threatened. The illustrations, which are more numerous and less apposite than comports with the dignity of history, may be imputed to the publishers, for publishers seek to attract readers whom authors would wish to repel; but it is to be feared that the page-headings—'Cruel habitations', 'If winter comes', and so forth—are the historian's.

These eight years of Louis Napoleon's life were so much fuller of events than the preceding forty that the second volume is a good deal longer than the first. Yet it might with advantage have been longer still. For an historian of this reign Mr Simpson spends perhaps too much time abroad but certainly too little at home. The Crimea, where Napoleon, to humour the English Government, did not appear in person, and the Europe of diplomacy, fill most of the pages after once the Emperor is seated on his throne. But the chief event of the time was what Mr Simpson calls in his title 'the recovery of France'. Social reforms and a wise internal administration were the Empire's best gifts to the country, and were not cancelled by its fall; and though Mr Simpson duly mentions and briefly enumerates these measures, they deserve to be explained in detail and shown in the working. It was the French people's gratitude to their tyrant which enabled him to wage unpopular wars in the interests of foreigners. His friendship for England and his sentimental affection for Italy and Germany were injurious and finally disastrous to his subjects: not so his compassion for the poor and his endeavours to alleviate the common lot of man. Henry IV had earned a name for benevolence by the inexpensive wish that every peasant should have a fowl in his pot: Napoleon III did his best to put it there.

The task of a fair and temperate historian, in treating of one who attracted so much spite and calumny, is a task of rehabilitation; and Mr Simpson, without resorting to advocacy, dispels much malevolent fiction by contrasting it with reality. Every new fact, every substitution of truth for falsehood, redounds to Napoleon's credit. For instance, it has been repeated, oftener than anything true is ever repeated, that he manoeuvred England into the Crimean war to be revenged on Nicholas I for a personal slight, to obtain admission on equal terms among European sovereigns, and to distract his enslaved countrymen from the contemplation of their chains. His countrymen were contented and pacific, and the war endangered his popularity; he made many efforts and some sacrifice of dignity to avert it; and it was forced upon Europe by the intrigues of a British ambassador, the stiffness of the Czar, and the bellicose temper of the English people and especially of their radical journalists.

It is fitting that amends should thus be made by an English historian to this ruler of France, for those amends are a national debt. That the Emperor should have enemies among the French was inevitable: he had deprived many professional politicians of their livelihood, and bereaved many orators of the sound of their own voice; and he was to this extent a tyrant, that he strictly repressed the minority opposed to his rule,—a minority comprising many who approved both his aims and his measures, but nevertheless were bound to oppose him because he was Count neither of Chambord nor of Paris. There was no such cause or excuse for the detestation of his person and government which was felt and expressed in our own happy, constitutional, and censorious country. Queen Victoria had ascended her throne without saying by your leave or with your leave; one house of Parliament was hereditary, and five-sixths of the adult male population had no voice in electing the other. These were the people who talked about despotism when a neighbouring nation, by universal suffrage and enormous majorities, had settled its own form of government. Though in truth it was not the English people but the enlightened English Liberals, then at the beginning of their long ascendancy, to whom the Emperor was odious; and the reason why they called him a despot was that he had put a despotism down, and had delivered France from the tyranny of Paris. The divine right of 2,000,000 Radicals to govern 30,000,000 Conservatives had been trampled underfoot; and Napoleon's chief offence in our country was this great service which he had rendered to his own. He left France diminished in territory and weakened in the face of Europe; but the eighteen years of his rule had at least cut the claws of the capital. When in 1871 Paris tried her last struggle with France, it was no longer dominion that she claimed, but only independence, and even independence was denied her; and those who had prated about the blood-stained origin of the Second Empire, and had dignified with the name of massacre the street-accident of Dec. 4, 1851, were taught what a massacre really is, and how much more blood it takes to found a republic than an empire.

One count in the British indictment against him was his private life, which was certainly dissolute; perhaps as dissolute as the Duke of Wellington's. I have been told by those who remembered his first visit to Windsor, in 1855, that the public was agitated, more furiously than the newspapers record, by the knowledge or belief that sovereigns embrace when they meet, and by rage and horror at the notion that 'those lips' should be allowed to sully the pure cheek of England's Queen. England's Queen, who had been kissed by her uncles, did not turn a hair; and a few months later, when Victor Emmanuel was the visitor and nobody made any fuss, the exemplary matron must have been pained to discover that her subjects' solicitude for the purity of her cheek was not sincere.

In this volume Mr Simpson has to deal with the two matters which supplied the Emperor's adversaries with their favourite themes: his broken oath to the Republic, and the famous massacre. On the former he has some excellent casuistry (in the proper sense of a word which Pascal and the Jesuits between them have brought into undeserved discredit), which may be cited here because it is also a characteristic piece of writing: pp. 170 f.

Oath-breaking is bad. But it is an altogether fortunate thing that oaths of allegiance have no worse effect than to exclude from political life a few abnormally honest men. Else all constitutional change would long ago have been rendered universally impossible, by the simple device of confining political life to the oath-bound. From this fate men's readiness to break oaths, and not their reluctance to impose them, has saved the world. Even though it knows them frangible few governments can resist the desire for the fictitious sense of security attained by the imposition of oaths of allegiance. But were such oaths really unbreakable no government could be deterred from what would then be a frantic eagerness to extort a genuine pledge of immortality. That there may never be lacking a supply of men willing at a pinch to break such oaths is the humiliating but manifest interest of mankind.

As for the affair of December 4, when the soldiery lost their heads and fired among the sight-seers, Mr Simpson condemns Napoleon because he profited by it, which is doubtful, and because he did not punish it; and he finds a parallel in William III's relation to the massacre of Glencoe. But the sight-seers had been warned by proclamation to stay at home; and from that point of view Napoleon may be held less responsible for their fate, not only than William III for the slaughter of the Macdonalds, but than William IV for the lamented death of Huskisson; for William IV had issued no proclamation advising ex-Presidents of the Board of Trade not to stand in front of railway trains.

17. KEATS'S 'THE FALL OF HYPERION', I 97 (1924)[17]

A letter to the Editor of 'The Times'

This poem was not printed in Keats's lifetime, and his manuscript has been lost; but in the copy made under the direction of Woodhouse lines 97–101 of the first canto run as follows:

> When in mid-way the sickening east wind
> Shifts sudden to the south, the small warm rain
> Melts out the frozen incense from all flowers,
> And fills the air with so much pleasant health
> That even the dying man forgets his shroud.

When an east wind shifts to the south, whether 'in mid-way', whatever that may be taken to mean, or 'in mid-day', as Lord Houghton printed, the result which is here described does not necessarily nor even usually follow. In order that rain may melt out incense from flowers, both flowers and incense must be there; and this condition is not fulfilled in any month between the autumnal and the vernal equinox. Such flowers as bloom in that half of the year are mostly scentless.

Keats wrote 'in mid-May', as in the 'Ode to a Nightingale' he wrote 'mid-May's eldest child'; and for confirmation the next lines are these:

> Even so that lofty sacrificial fire,
> Sending forth Maian incense, spread around
> Forgetfulness of everything but bliss.

18. DR FRAENKEL'S APPOINTMENT (1934)[18]

A letter to the Editor of 'The Sunday Times'

I have been asked by scholars at Oxford to answer a note by 'Atticus' on p. 13 of the *Sunday Times* of the 16th inst. concerning the election of Dr Eduard Fraenkel to the

Corpus Professorship of Latin, where he makes the shade (which he represents as indignant) of Conington (whom he describes as a great Latinist) inquire: 'Is, then, Oxford so barren in Latinity that she has to choose an ex-professor from Freiburg University to fill the chair and occupy the rooms which once were mine?'

The question is invidiously put, and would not have been put by Conington, who was a modest man; but 'Atticus' gives the answer in his next words: 'Herr Fraenkel is a Latinist of European reputation.' I do not know who the other candidates were, but they cannot have been Latinists of European reputation; for no Englishman who could be so described was young enough to be eligible.

IV

THE APPLICATION OF THOUGHT
TO TEXTUAL CRITICISM

The following paper[1] was read to the Classical Association meeting at Cambridge on 4 August 1921.

In beginning to speak about the application of thought to textual criticism, I do not intend to define the term *thought*, because I hope that the sense which I attach to the word will emerge from what I say. But it is necessary at the outset to define *textual criticism*, because many people, and even some people who profess to teach it to others, do not know what it is. One sees books calling themselves introductions to textual criticism which contain nothing about textual criticism from beginning to end; which are all about palaeography and manuscripts and collation, and have no more to do with textual criticism than if they were all about accidence and syntax. Palaeography is one of the things with which a textual critic needs to acquaint himself, but grammar is another, and equally indispensable; and no amount either of grammar or of palaeography will teach a man one scrap of textual criticism.

Textual criticism is a science, and, since it comprises recension and emendation, it is also an art. It is the science of discovering error in texts and the art of removing it. That is its definition, that is what the name *denotes*. But I must also say something about what it does and does not *connote*, what attributes it does and does not imply; because here also there are false impressions abroad.

First, then, it is not a sacred mystery. It is purely a matter of reason and of common sense. We exercise textual criticism whenever we notice and correct a misprint. A man who possesses common sense and the use of reason must not expect to learn from treatises or lectures on textual criticism anything that he could not, with leisure and industry, find out for himself. What the lectures and treatises can do for him is to save him time and trouble by presenting to him immediately considerations which would in any case occur to him sooner or later. And whatever he reads about textual criticism in books, or hears at lectures, he should test by reason and common sense, and reject everything which conflicts with either as mere hocus-pocus.

Secondly, textual criticism is not a branch of mathematics, nor indeed an exact science at all. It deals with a matter not rigid and constant, like lines and numbers, but fluid and variable; namely the frailties and aberrations of the human mind, and of its insubordinate servants, the human fingers. It therefore is not susceptible of hard-and-fast rules. It would be much easier if it were; and that is why people try to pretend that it is, or at least behave as if they thought so. Of course you can have hard-and-fast rules if you like, but then you will have false rules, and they will lead you wrong; because their simplicity will render them inapplicable to problems which are not simple, but complicated by the play of personality. A textual critic engaged upon his business is not at all like Newton investigating the motions of the planets: he is much more like a dog hunting for fleas. If a dog hunted for fleas on mathematical principles, basing his researches on statistics of area and population, he would never catch a flea except by accident. They require to be treated as individuals; and every problem which presents itself to the textual critic must be regarded as possibly unique.

Textual criticism therefore is neither mystery nor mathematics: it cannot be learnt either like the catechism or like the multiplication table. This science and this art require more in the learner than a simply receptive mind; and indeed the truth is that they cannot be taught at all: *criticus nascitur, non fit.* If a dog is to hunt for fleas success-fully he must be quick and he must be sensitive. It is no good for a rhinoceros to hunt for fleas: he does not know where they are, and could not catch them if he did. It has sometimes been said that textual criticism is the crown and summit of all scholarship. This is not evidently or necessarily true; but it is true that the qualities which make a critic, whether they are thus transcendent or no, are rare, and that a good critic is a much less common thing than for instance a good grammarian. I have in my mind a paper by a well-known scholar on a certain Latin writer, half of which was concerned with grammar and half with criticism. The grammatical part was excel-lent; it showed wide reading and accurate observation, and contributed matter which was both new and valuable. In the textual part the author was like nothing so much as an ill-bred child interrupting the conversation of grown men. If it was possible to mistake the question at issue, he mistook it. If an opponent's arguments were contained in some book which was not at hand, he did not try to find the book, but he tried to guess the arguments; and he never succeeded. If the book was at hand, and he had read the arguments, he did not understand them; and represented his opponents as saying the opposite of what they had said. If another scholar had already removed a corruption by slightly altering the text, he proposed to remove it by altering the text violently. So possible is it to be a learned man, and admirable in other departments, and yet to have in you not even the makings of a critic.

But the application of thought to textual criticism is an action which ought to be within the power of anyone who can apply thought to anything. It is not, like the talent for textual criticism, a gift of nature, but it is a habit; and, like other habits, it can be formed. And, when formed, although it cannot fill the place of an absent talent, it can modify and minimise the ill effects of the talent's absence. Because a man is not a born critic, he need not therefore act like a born fool; but when he engages in textual criticism he often does. There are reasons for everything, and there are reasons for this; and I will now set forth the chief of them. The *fact* that thought is not sufficiently applied to the subject I shall show hereafter by examples; but at present I consider the causes which bring that result about.

First, then, not only is a natural aptitude for the study rare, but so also is a genuine interest in it. Most people, and many scholars among them, find it rather dry and rather dull. Now if a subject bores us, we are apt to avoid the trouble of thinking about it; but if we do that, we had better go further and avoid also the trouble of writing about it. And that is what English scholars often did in the middle of the nineteenth century, when nobody in England wanted to hear about textual criticism. This was not an ideal condition of affairs, but it had its compensation. The less one says about a subject which one does not understand, the less one will say about it which is foolish; and on this subject editors were allowed by public opinion to be silent if they chose. But public opinion is now aware that textual criticism, however repulsive, is nevertheless indispensable, and editors find that some pretence of dealing with the subject is obligatory; and in these circumstances they apply, not thought, but words, to textual criticism. They get rules by rote without grasping the realities of which those rules are merely emblems, and recite them on inappropriate occasions instead of seriously thinking out each problem as it arises.

Secondly, it is only a minority of those who engage in this study who are sincerely bent upon the discovery of truth. We all know that the discovery of truth is seldom the sole object of political writers; and the world believes, justly or unjustly, that it is not always the sole object of theologians: but the amount of sub-conscious dishonesty which pervades the textual criticism of the Greek and Latin classics is little suspected except by those who have had occasion to analyse it. People come upon this field bringing with them prepossessions and preferences; they are not willing to look all facts in the face, nor to draw the most probable conclusion unless it is also the most agreeable conclusion. Most men are rather stupid, and most of those who are not stupid are, consequently, rather vain; and it is hardly possible to step aside from the pursuit of truth without falling a victim either to your stupidity or else to your vanity. Stupidity will then attach you to received opinions, and you will stick in the mud; or vanity will set you hunting for novelty, and you will find mare's nests. Added to these snares and hindrances there are the various forms of partisanship: sectarianism, which handcuffs you to your own school and teachers and associates, and patriotism which handcuffs you to your own country. Patriotism has a great name as a virtue, and in civic matters, at the present stage of the world's history, it possibly still does more good than harm; but in the sphere of the intellect it is an unmitigated nuisance. I do not know which cuts the worse figure: a German scholar encouraging his countrymen to believe that 'wir Deutsche' have nothing to learn from foreigners, or an Englishman demonstrating the unity of Homer by sneers at 'Teutonic professors', who are supposed by his audience to have goggle eyes behind large spectacles, and ragged moustaches saturated in lager beer, and consequently to be incapable of forming literary judgments.

Thirdly, these internal causes of error and folly are subject to very little counteraction or correction from outside. The average reader knows hardly anything about textual criticism, and therefore cannot exercise a vigilant control over the writer: the addle-pate is at liberty to maunder and the impostor is at liberty to lie. And, what is worse, the reader often shares the writer's prejudices, and is far too well pleased with his conclusions to examine either his premises or his reasoning. Stand on a barrel in the streets of Bagdad, and say in a loud voice, 'Twice two is four, and ginger is hot in the mouth, therefore Mohammed is the prophet of God', and your logic will probably escape criticism; or, if anyone by chance should criticise it, you could easily silence him by calling him a Christian dog.

Fourthly, the things which the textual critic has to talk about are not things which present themselves clearly and sharply to the mind; and it is easy to say, and to fancy that you think, what you really do not think, and even what, if you seriously tried to think it, you would find to be unthinkable. Mistakes are therefore made which could not be made if the matter under discussion were any corporeal object, having qualities perceptible to the senses. The human senses have had a much longer history than the human intellect, and have been brought much nearer to perfection: they are far more acute, far less easy to deceive. The difference between an icicle and a red-hot poker is really much slighter than the difference between truth and falsehood or sense and nonsense; yet it is much more immediately noticeable and much more universally noticed, because the body is more sensitive than the mind. I find therefore that a good way of exposing the falsehood of a statement or the absurdity of an argument in textual criticism is to transpose it into sensuous terms and see what it looks like then. If the nouns which we use are the names of things which can be handled or tasted, differing from one another in being hot or cold, sweet or sour, then we realise what we are saying and take care what we say. But the terms of textual criticism are deplorably intellectual; and probably in no other field do men tell so many falsehoods in the idle hope that they are telling the truth, or talk so much nonsense in the vague belief that they are talking sense.

This is particularly unfortunate and particularly reprehensible, because there is no science in which it is more necessary to take precautions against error arising from internal causes. Those who follow the physical sciences enjoy the great advantage that they can constantly bring their opinions to the test of fact, and verify or falsify their theories by experiment. When a chemist has mixed sulphur and saltpetre and charcoal in certain proportions and wishes to ascertain if the mixture is explosive, he need only apply a match. When a doctor has compounded a new drug and desires to find out what diseases, if any, it is good for, he has only to give it to his patients all round and notice which die and which recover. Our conclusions regarding the truth or falsehood of a MS. reading can never be confirmed or corrected by an equally decisive test; for the only equally decisive test would be the production of the author's autograph. The discovery merely of better and older MSS. than were previously known to us is *not* equally decisive; and even this inadequate verification is not to be expected often, or on a large scale. It is therefore a matter of common prudence and common decency that we should neglect no safeguard lying within our reach; that we should look sharp after ourselves; that we should narrowly scrutinise our own proceedings and rigorously analyse our springs of action. How far these elementary requirements are satisfied, we will now learn from examples.

At the very beginning, to see what pure irrelevancy, what almost incredible foolishness, finds its way into print, take this instance. It had been supposed for several centuries that Plautus' name was *M. Accius Plautus*, when Ritschl in 1845 pointed out that in the Ambrosian palimpsest discovered by Mai in 1815, written in the fourth or fifth century, and much the oldest of Plautus' MSS., the name appears in the genitive as *T. Macci Plauti*, so that he was really called *Titus Maccius* (or *Maccus*) *Plautus*. An Italian scholar, one Vallauri, objected to this innovation on the ground that in all printed editions from the sixteenth to the nineteenth century the name was *M. Accius*. He went to Milan to look at the palimpsest, and there, to be sure, he found *T. Macci* quite legibly written. But he observed that many *other* pages of the MS. were quite illegible, and that the whole book was very much tattered and battered; whereupon he said that he could not sufficiently wonder at anyone attaching any weight to a MS. which was in such a condition. Is there any other science, anything calling itself a science, into which such intellects intrude and conduct such operations in public? But you may think that Mr Vallauri is a unique phenomenon. No: if you engage in textual criticism you may come upon a second Mr Vallauri at any turn. The MSS. of Catullus, none of them older than the fourteenth century, present at 64 23 the verse:

> heroes saluete, deum genus! o bona mater!

The Veronese scholia on Virgil, a palimpsest of the fifth or sixth century, at *Aen*. v 80, 'salue sancte parens', have the note: 'Catullus: saluete, deum *gens*, o bona *matrum* | progenies, saluete iter[um]'—giving *gens* for *genus*, *matrum* for *mater*, and adding a half-verse absent from Catullus' MSS.; and scholars have naturally preferred an authority so much more ancient. But one editor is found to object: 'the weight of the Veronese scholia, imperfect and full of lacunae as they are, is not to be set against our MSS.' There is Mr Vallauri over again: because the palimpsest has large holes elsewhere and because much of it has perished, therefore what remains, though written as early as the sixth century, has less authority than MSS. written in the fourteenth. If however anyone gets hold of these fourteenth-century MSS., destroys pages of them and tears holes in the pages he does not destroy, the authority of those parts which he allows to survive will presumably deteriorate, and may even sink as low as that of the palimpsest.

Again. There are two MSS. of a certain author, which we will call *A* and *B*. Of these two it is recognised that *A* is the more correct but the less sincere, and that *B* is the more corrupt but the less interpolated. It is desired to know which MS., if either, is better than the other, or whether both are equal. One scholar tries to determine this question by the collection and comparison of examples. But another thinks that he knows a shorter way than that; and it consists in saying 'the more sincere MS. is and must be for any critic who understands his business the better MS.'

This I cite as a specimen of the things which people may say if they do not think about the meaning of what they are saying, and especially as an example of the danger of dealing in generalisations. The best way to treat such pretentious inanities is to transfer them from the sphere of textual criticism, where the difference between truth and falsehood or between sense and nonsense is little regarded and seldom even perceived, into some sphere where men are obliged to use concrete and sensuous terms, which force them, however reluctantly, to think.

I ask this scholar, this critic who knows his business, and who says that the more sincere of two MSS. is and must be the better—I ask him to tell me which weighs most, a tall man or a fat man. He cannot answer; nobody can; everybody sees in a moment that the question is absurd. *Tall* and *fat* are adjectives which transport even a textual critic from the world of humbug into the world of reality, a world inhabited by comparatively thoughtful people, such as butchers and grocers, who depend on their brains for their bread. There he begins to understand that to such general questions any answer must be false; that judgment can only be pronounced on individual specimens; that everything depends on the degree of tallness and the degree of fatness. It may well be that an inch of girth adds more weight than an inch of height, or *vice versa*; but that altitude is incomparably more ponderous than obesity, or obesity than altitude, and that an inch of one depresses the scale more than a yard of the other, has never been maintained. The way to find out whether this tall man weighs more or less than that fat man is to weigh them; and the way to find out whether this corrupt MS. is better or worse than that interpolated MS. is to collect and compare their readings; not to ride easily off on the false and ridiculous generalisation that the more sincere MS. is and must be the better.

When you call a MS. *sincere* you instantly engage on its behalf the moral sympathy of the thoughtless: moral sympathy is a line in which they are very strong. I do not desire to exclude morality from textual criticism; I wish indeed that some moral qualities were commoner in textual criticism than they are; but let us not indulge our moral emotions out of season. It may be that a scribe who interpolates, who makes changes deliberately, is guilty of wickedness, while a scribe who makes changes accidentally, because he is sleepy or illiterate or drunk, is guilty of none; but that is a question which will be determined by a competent authority at the Day of Judgment, and is no concern of ours. Our concern is not with the eternal destiny of the scribe, but with the temporal utility of the MS.; and a MS. is useful or the reverse in proportion to the amount of truth which it discloses or conceals, no matter what may be the causes of the disclosure or concealment. It is a mistake to suppose that deliberate change is always or necessarily more destructive of truth than accidental change; and even if it were, the main question, as I have said already, is one of degree. A MS. in which 1 per cent of the words have been viciously and intentionally altered and 99 per cent are right is not so bad as a MS. in which only 1 per cent are right and 99 per cent have been altered virtuously and unintentionally; and if you go to a critic with any such vague enquiry as the question whether the 'more sincere' or the 'more correct' of two MSS. is the better, he will reply, 'If I am to answer that question, you must show me the two MSS. first; for aught that I know at present, from the terms of your query, either may be better than the other, or both may be equal.' But that is what the incompetent

intruders into criticism can never admit. They *must* have
a better MS., whether it exists or no; because they could
never get along without one. If Providence permitted
two MSS. to be equal, the editor would have to choose
between their readings by considerations of intrinsic merit,
and in order to do that he would need to acquire intelligence and impartiality and willingness to take pains, and
all sorts of things which he neither has nor wishes for;
and he feels sure that God, who tempers the wind to the
shorn lamb, can never have meant to lay upon his shoulders
such a burden as this.

This is thoughtlessness in the sphere of recension: come
now to the sphere of emendation. There is one foolish
sort of conjecture which seems to be commoner in the
British Isles than anywhere else, though it is also practised
abroad, and of late years especially at Munich. The practice is, if you have persuaded yourself that a text is corrupt,
to alter a letter or two and see what happens. If what
happens is anything which the warmest good-will can
mistake for sense and grammar, you call it an emendation;
and you call this silly game the palaeographical method.

The palaeographical method has always been the delight
of tiros and the scorn of critics. Haupt, for example, used
to warn his pupils against mistaking this sort of thing for
emendation. 'The prime requisite of a good emendation',
said he, 'is that it should start from the thought; it
is only afterwards that other considerations, such as those
of metre, or possibilities, such as the interchange of letters,
are taken into account.' And again: 'If the sense requires it, I am prepared to write *Constantinopolitanus* where
the MSS. have the monosyllabic interjection *o*.' And again:
'From the requirement that one should always begin with
the thought, there results, as is self-evident, the negative
aspect of the case, that one should not, at the outset,

consider what exchange of letters may possibly have brought about the corruption of the passage one is dealing with.' And further, in his oration on Lachmann as a critic: 'Some people, if they see that anything in an ancient text wants correcting, immediately betake themselves to the art of palaeography, investigate the shapes of letters and the forms of abbreviation, and try one dodge after another, as if it were a game, until they hit upon something which they think they can substitute for the corruption; as if forsooth truth were generally discovered by shots of that sort, or as if emendation could take its rise from anything but a careful consideration of the thought.'

But even when palaeography is kept in her proper place, as handmaid, and not allowed to give herself the airs of mistress, she is apt to be overworked. There is a preference for conjectures which call in the aid of palaeography, and which assume, as the cause of error, the accidental interchange of similar letters or similar words, although other causes of error are known to exist. One is presented, for instance, with the following maxim:

Interpolation is, speaking generally, comparatively an uncommon source of alteration, and we should therefore be loth to assume it in a given case.

Every case is a given case; so what this maxim really means is that we should always be loth to assume interpolation as a source of alteration. But it is certain, and admitted by this writer when he uses the phrase 'comparatively uncommon', that interpolation does occur; so he is telling us that we should be loth to assume interpolation even when that assumption is true. And the reason why we are to behave in this ridiculous manner is that interpolation is, speaking generally, comparatively an uncommon source of alteration.

Now to detect a *non sequitur*, unless it leads to an unwelcome conclusion, is as much beyond the power of the average reader as it is beyond the power of the average writer to attach ideas to his own words when those words are terms of textual criticism. I will therefore substitute other terms, terms to which ideas must be attached; and I invite consideration of this maxim and this ratiocination:

A bullet-wound is, speaking generally, comparatively an uncommon cause of death, and we should therefore be loth to assume it in a given case.

Should we? Should we be loth to assume a bullet-wound as the cause of death if the given case were death on a battlefield? and should we be loth to do so for the reason alleged, that a bullet-wound is, speaking generally, comparatively an uncommon cause of death? Ought we to assume instead the commonest cause of death, and assign death on a battlefield to tuberculosis? What would be thought of a counsellor who enjoined that method of procedure? Well, it would probably be thought that he was a textual critic strayed from home.

Why is interpolation comparatively uncommon? For the same reason that bullet-wounds are: because the opportunity for it is comparatively uncommon. Interpolation is provoked by real or supposed difficulties, and is not frequently volunteered where all is plain sailing; whereas accidental alteration may happen anywhere. Every letter of every word lies exposed to it, and that is the sole reason why accidental alteration is more common. In a given case where either assumption is possible, the assumption of interpolation is equally probable, nay more probable; because action with a motive is more probable than action without a motive. The truth therefore is that in such a case we should be loth to assume accident and should rather assume interpolation; and the circumstance that such cases are comparatively uncommon is no reason for behaving irrationally when they occur.

There is one special province of textual criticism, a large and important province, which is concerned with the establishment of rules of grammar and of metre. Those rules are in part traditional, and given us by the ancient grammarians; but in part they are formed by our own induction from what we find in the MSS. of Greek and Latin authors; and even the traditional rules must of course be tested by comparison with the witness of the MSS. But every rule, whether traditional or framed from induction, is sometimes broken by the MSS.; it may be by few, it may be by many; it may be seldom, it may be often; and critics may then say that the MSS. are wrong, and may correct them in accordance with the rule. This state of affairs is apparently, nay evidently, paradoxical. The MSS. are the material upon which we base our rule, and then, when we have got our rule, we turn round upon the MSS. and say that the rule, based upon them, convicts them of error. We are thus working in a circle, that is a fact which there is no denying; but, as Lachmann says, the task of the critic is just this, to tread that circle deftly and warily; and that is precisely what elevates the critic's business above mere mechanical labour. The difficulty is one which lies in the nature of the case, and is inevitable: and the only way to surmount it is just to be a critic.

The paradox is more formidable in appearance than in reality, and has plenty of analogies in daily life. In a trial or lawsuit the jury's verdict is mainly based upon the evidence of the witnesses; but that does not prevent the jury from making up its mind, from the evidence in general, that one or more witnesses have been guilty of perjury and that their evidence is to be disregarded.

It is quite possible to elicit from the general testimony of MSS. a rule of sufficient certainty to convict of falsehood their exceptional testimony, or of sufficient probability to throw doubt upon it. But that exceptional testimony must in each case be considered. It must be recognised that there are two hypotheses between which we have to decide: the question is whether the exceptions come from the author, and so break down the rule, or whether they come from the scribe, and are to be corrected by it: and in order to decide this we must keep our eyes open for any peculiarity which may happen to characterise them.

One of the forms which lack of thought has assumed in textual criticism is the tendency now prevailing, especially among some Continental scholars, to try to break down accepted rules of grammar or metre by the mere collection and enumeration of exceptions presented by the MSS. Now that can never break down a rule: the mere number of exceptions is nothing; what matters is their weight, and that can only be ascertained by classification and scrutiny. If I had noted down every example which I have met, I should now have a large collection of places in Latin MSS. where the substantive *orbis*, which our grammars and dictionaries declare to be masculine, has a feminine adjective attached to it. But I do not therefore propose to revise that rule of syntax, for examination would show that these examples, though numerous, have no force. Most of them are places where the sense and context show that *orbis*, in whatever case or number it may be, is merely a corruption of the corresponding case and number of *urbs*; and in the remaining places it is natural to suppose that the scribe has been influenced and confused by the great likeness of the one word to the other. Or again, read Madvig, *Adu. Crit.*, vol. i, book i, chap. iv, where he sifts the evidence for the opinion that the

aorist infinitive can be used in Greek after verbs of saying
and thinking in the sense of the future infinitive or of the
aorist infinitive with ἄν. The list of examples in the MSS.
is very long indeed; but the moment you begin to sort
them and examine them you are less struck by their
number than by the restriction of their extent. Almost
all of them are such as δέξασθαι used for δέξεσθαι, where
the two forms differ by one letter only; a smaller number
are such as ποιῆσαι for ποιήσειν, where the difference,
though greater, is still slight; others are examples like
ἥκιστα ἀναγκασθῆναι for ἥκιστ' ἂν ἀναγκασθῆναι, where
again the difference is next to nothing. Now if the MSS.
are right in these cases, and the Greek authors did use this
construction, how are we to explain this extraordinary
limitation of the use? There is no syntactical difference
between the first and second aorist: why then did they
use the 1st aorist so often for the future and the 2nd
aorist so seldom? why did they say δέξασθαι for δέξεσθαι
dozens of times and λαβεῖν for λήψεσθαι never? The
mere asking of that question is enough to show the true
state of the case. The bare fact that the aorists thus used
in the MSS. are aorists of similar *form* to the future, while
aorists of dissimilar form are not thus used, proves that
the phenomenon has its cause in the copyist's eye and not
in the author's mind, that it is not a variation in grammatical usage but an error in transcription. The number
of examples is nothing; all depends upon their character;
and a single example of λαβεῖν in a future sense would
have more weight than a hundred of δέξασθαι.

In particular, scribes will alter a less familiar form to
a more familiar, if they see nothing to prevent them. If
metre allows, or if they do not know that metre forbids,
they will alter ἐλεινός to ἐλεεινός, οἰστός to ὀϊστός, *nil* to
nihil, *deprendo* to *deprehendo*. Since metre convicts them of

infidelity in some places, they forfeit the right to be trusted in any place; if we choose to trust them we are credulous, and if we build structures on our trust we are no critics. Even if metre does not convict them, reason sometimes can. Take the statement, repeatedly made in grammars and editions, that the Latins sometimes used the pluperfect for the imperfect and the perfect. They did use it for the imperfect; they used it also for the preterite or past aorist; but for the perfect they did not use it; and that is proved by the very examples of its use as perfect which are found in MSS. All those examples are of the 3rd person plural. Why? We must choose between the two following hypotheses:

(*a*) That the Latins used the pluperfect for the perfect in the 3rd person plural only.

(*b*) That they did not use the pluperfect for the perfect, and that these examples are corrupt.

If anyone adopted the former, he would have to explain what syntactical property, inviting the author to use pluperfect for perfect, is possessed by the 3rd person plural and not by the two other plural or the three singular persons: and I should like to see some one set about it.

If we adopt the latter, we must show what *external* feature, inviting the *scribe* to write pluperfect for perfect, is possessed by the 3rd person plural exclusively: and that is quite easy. The 3rd person plural is the only person in which the perfect and the pluperfect differ merely by one letter. Moreover in verse the perfect termination -*ĕrunt*, being comparatively unfamiliar to scribes, is altered by them to the nearest familiar form with the same scansion, sometimes -*erint*, sometimes -*erant*: in Ovid's *Heroides* there are four places where the best MS. gives *praebuĕrunt, stetĕrunt, excidĕrunt, expulĕrunt,* and the other MSS. give -*erant* or -*erint* or both. Accordingly, when the much inferior MSS. of Propertius present pluperfect for perfect in four places, *fuerant* once, *steterant* once, *exciderant* twice, Scaliger corrects to *fuĕrunt, stetĕrunt, excidĕrunt*. Thereupon an editor of this enlightened age takes up his pen and writes as follows: 'It is quite erroneous to remove the pluperfects where it can be done without great expenditure of conjectural sagacity (*steterunt* for *steterant* and the like), and not to trouble oneself about the phenomenon elsewhere.' I ask, how is it possible to trouble oneself about the phenomenon elsewhere? It does not exist elsewhere. There is no place where the MSS. give *steteram* in the sense of the perfect *steti*, nor *steteras* in the sense of the perfect *stetisti*. Wherever they give examples of the pluperfect which cannot be removed by the change of one letter— such as *pararat* in i 8 36 or *fueram* in i 12 11—those are examples where it has sometimes the sense of the imperfect, sometimes of the preterite, but never of the perfect. And the inference is plain: the Latins did not use the pluperfect for the perfect.

Scaliger knew that in the sixteenth century: Mr Rothstein, in the nineteenth and twentieth, does not know it; he has found a form of words to prevent him from knowing it, and he thinks himself in advance of Scaliger. It is supposed that there has been progress in the science of textual criticism, and the most frivolous pretender has learnt to talk superciliously about 'the old unscientific days'. The old unscientific days are everlasting; they are here and now; they are renewed perennially by the ear which takes formulas in, and the tongue which gives them out again, and the mind which meanwhile is empty of reflexion and stuffed with self-complacency. Progress there has been, but where? In superior intellects: the rabble do not share it. Such a man as Scaliger, living in our time, would be a better critic than Scaliger was; but we shall not be better critics than Scaliger by the simple act of living in our own time. Textual criticism, like most other sciences, is an aristocratic affair, not communicable to all men, nor to most men. Not to be a textual critic is no reproach to anyone, unless he pretends to be what he is not. To *be* a textual critic requires aptitude for thinking and willingness to think; and though it also requires other things, those things are supplements and cannot be substitutes. Knowledge is good, method is good, but one thing beyond all others is necessary; and that is to have a head, not a pumpkin, on your shoulders, and brains, not pudding, in your head.

V

BIOGRAPHICAL

I. J. M. IMAGE (1919)[1]

JOHN Maxwell Image was born, the elder son of the Rev. John Image, at St Leonard's in Sussex on May 16th (not May 11th as stated in *Admissions to Trinity College*) 1842. From Brighton College he came up in February 1861 to Trinity, where he was elected to a minor scholarship in the same year and to a scholarship in 1863. He was a sound and elegant classic, notably skilled in composition, and was bracketed second with R. Durnford in the Tripos of Whitelaw's year 1865; he also won in 1864 the Browne Scholarship and the Browne's Medal for a Greek epigram. In 1867 he was elected Fellow of his College, where from 1869 to 1893 he served on the teaching staff as Lecturer in Classics, and was Tutor from 1875 to 1885, discharging his office with efficiency and success. His pupils remember him as one who showed even more than the usual concern of a Tutor for their welfare and improvement. He would enumerate and press on their notice the various sports which Cambridge offered to their choice as antidotes to her climate: they ranged through a descending scale from the royal game of tennis to the exercise, not then extinct, of walking. The correct mode of addressing a letter was also inculcated, with illustrations on the blackboard in his beautiful handwriting. In his earlier days he rendered service much valued by his colleagues as an exact and judicious examiner for scholarships and fellowships; but about his fortieth year he began to excuse himself from such work, alleging that he had lost nerve, and between the end of his tutorship and his retirement from the teaching staff in 1893 he lectured only to passmen. This diffidence was the growth and excess of a natural modesty and reserve which belonged to the very essence of his character. No shyness was visible in his manner: his address was winning and hearty, and he conversed with ease and liveliness; but he did not seek society, and his sincere and affectionate nature found its greatest happiness among a few intimate friends. The chief of these was Mr W. F. Smith of St John's College, with whom he formed in his undergraduate days a friendship uninterruptedly maintained, with a weekly interchange of letters, to the end of his life. It is Mr Smith who should rightly have written this notice, but he was attacked by illness almost at the moment when his friend died.

In early life Image had circumnavigated the globe, and he once paid a visit to the West Indies to look after some property there; but otherwise he seldom if ever travelled beyond England. It was an amusing instance of his reserve that he chose to keep up the old fashion—dating from times when the tenure of Fellowships depended on celibacy and Fellows lived half the year in retired spots with their clandestine wives—of reticence about absences from Cambridge. Those who asked him where he had been spending the long vacation would be recalled to discretion by the answer, 'I have been staying in the country.' Next to his college, which he was accustomed to magnify at the expense of all colleges wheresoever situate, and upon which, as he would relate with pride, he had conferred the benefaction of persuading the Seniority to sanction smoking in the Small Combination Room, the chief centres of his interest were the Military and Naval

Services; and his acquaintance with their history and customs was such as few civilians possess.

The happy marriage which he contracted in 1915 withdrew him much from the common life of the Society. If one reproached him with never dining in Hall, he would plead in excuse the distance of his house, the season of the year, and the double darkness which at that time was shed upon Cambridge by the prince of the power of the air. But the days grew longer and his appearances in Hall grew no more frequent; till it became quite clear that he was fonder of his own hearth than a cenobite has any business to be. He made a new circle of friends among his immediate neighbours; and the Barton Road gave him more scope than Isaac Newton's rooms in the Old Court for indulging his love of children, to whom he was a devoted playfellow, and would take incredible pains—only they were no pains to him—for their delight and entertainment. His death at seventy-seven was a surprise as well as a grief to his friends, for both in looks and in spirit he was a younger man than his years. On the morning of Sunday, November 2nd, he complained of a pain across the chest, but the suggestion that he should stay at home instead of attending the Memorial Service in the College Chapel dispelled it instantly, and he walked firmly and briskly to Trinity. The scene and the occasion told upon his feelings, and when he left the Chapel his emotion was such that it was some ten minutes before he could be allowed to start for home. Throughout the afternoon and evening he was as cheerful and seemed as well as usual; but he had only just retired to rest when there was a sudden failure of the heart's action, and in three minutes all was over. On November 7th, after a service in the College Chapel, he was buried at Grantchester.

2. ARTHUR PLATT (1927)

The author of the papers collected in this volume[2] was one whose published writings, though they show the rare quality of his mind, do not portray the range of his studies and the variety of his accomplishments. Nor do these papers themselves complete the picture; but they have been recovered and put together that the world may know a little more of an uncommonly gifted man who was not much before its eye, and whose reputation was highest within the narrower circle which knew him well enough to admire him rightly.

It is not certain that he would have consented to their publication, for he must have felt that they bear some traces of the circumstances which called them forth. University College London, like many other colleges, is the abode of a Minotaur. This monster does not devour youths and maidens: it consists of them, and it preys for choice on the Professors within its reach. It is called a Literary Society, and in hopes of deserving the name it exacts a periodical tribute from those whom it supposes to be literate. Studious men who might be settling *Hoti's* business and properly basing *Oun* are expected to provide amusing discourses on subjects of which they have no official knowledge and upon which they may not be entitled even to open their mouths. Platt, whose temper made him accessible, whose pen ran easily, and whose mind was richly stored, paid more of this blackmail than most of his colleagues, and grudged it less; but the fact is not to be concealed that these unconstrained and even exuberant essays were written to order. The only one which he allowed to be printed, and that only in a college magazine, is *Aristophanes*. Two however have a different origin and were composed with more deliberation. *Science and Arts among the Ancients* is an address delivered before the Faculties of Arts and Science in University College on a ceremonial occasion, the opening of the Session in October 1899; and the Prelection is one of those read in public by the candidates for the Cambridge Chair of Greek when it fell vacant in 1921.

John Arthur, eldest of the fourteen children of Francis Thomas Platt, was born in London on the 11th of July 1860 and died at Bournemouth on the 16th of March 1925. He was sent to school at Harrow, whence he went up to Cambridge in 1879, winning a scholarship at Trinity College. In the first part of the Classical Tripos of 1882 he was placed in the second division of the first class, a position which may have disappointed himself but did not surprise those friends who, whenever they went into his rooms, had found him deep in books which had no bearing on the examination. In the second part a year later he obtained a first class in Literature and Criticism and also in Ancient Philosophy. In 1884, like his father and grandfather before him, he was elected a Fellow of Trinity. This Fellowship he lost under the old statutes by his marriage in 1885 with Mildred Barham, daughter of Sir Edward Bond, K.C.B., sometime Librarian of the British Museum, and granddaughter of R. H. Barham, the author of the *Ingoldsby Legends*. Their children were one son and one daughter. For the next eight years he taught at the coaching establishment of Wren and Gurney in Bayswater; in 1894 he was chosen to succeed his friend William Wyse as Professor of Greek in University College London, and soon after took up his residence about a mile away on the edge of Regent's Park. He held his Professorship more than 30 years. In 1921, when Henry Jackson died, he was persuaded to become a candidate for the Chair of Greek at Cambridge, to which few or none of the competitors had a juster claim; but he was relieved when he was not elected, and it is certain that Cambridge would have been less to his taste than London as a place to live in. He would have vacated his office at University College by reason of age in July 1925, but in 1924 he was attacked by illness, and did not live to complete his term.

At the time of his appointment some feared that they were yoking a racehorse to the plough and that his duties might be irksome to him because they could hardly be interesting. Much of the teaching which he was required to give was elementary, and he seldom had pupils who possessed a native aptitude for classical studies or intended to pursue them far. But he proved assiduous, patient, and effective: only an oaf could help learning from him and liking him; and with his best students he formed enduring ties, and would inveigle them into reading Dante or Cervantes with him at his house of an evening after they had taken their degrees. Outside his own class-room he was a centre and fount of the general life of the College, most of all in the Musical Society and among his colleagues in the smoking-room after luncheon. Nearer to his house he made another circle of friends. He was a Fellow of the Zoological Society, frequented its Gardens, and inspired a romantic passion in their resident population. There was a leopard which at Platt's approach would almost ooze through the bars of its cage to establish contact with the beloved object; the gnu, if it saw him on the opposite side of its broad enclosure, would walk all the way across to have its fore-lock pulled; and a credible witness reports the following scene.

I remember going to the giraffe-house and seeing a crowd of children watching a man who had removed his hat while the giraffe, its neck stretched to the fullest capacity, was rubbing its head backwards and forwards upon the bald crown. When the object of this somewhat embarrassing affection turned his head, Platt's features were revealed.

In youth he had poetical ambitions, and his first book was a volume of verse; a smaller one on a personal theme was printed privately, and so was a collection, made after his death, of sonnets, very personal indeed, with which he had entertained and striven to ameliorate his colleagues. He early produced recensions of the *Odyssey* and the *Iliad*, in which it was his aim to restore, so far as might be, the original language of the poet or poets, and thus to pursue further that special line of Homeric study which began with Bentley and his digamma, engaged the acute but undisciplined minds of Payne Knight and Brandreth, and has left as memorials of its progress the editions of Bekker and of Nauck. Nothing could be more different, or could better display his versatility, than his other chief work, the translation of Aristotle's *De generatione animalium* with its multifarious notes on matters zoological. A slighter performance was a free rendering of the *Agamemnon* of Aeschylus into the prose of King James's Bible.

Among the Greek scholars of his country Platt belonged to that company of explorers whose leading figures, after the universal genius of Bentley, are Dawes, Porson, and Elmsley. Minute and refined observation for the ascertainment of grammatical and metrical usage was his chosen province; and his early investigations of Homeric practice were his most characteristic work, and probably surpass in value his later and more various contributions to interpretation and textual criticism. Metrical science, upon the death of Elmsley, had deserted its native isle and taken flight to the Continent: Platt was one of the very few Englishmen who in the last hundred years have advanced the study, and among those few he was the foremost. In conjectural emendation, like Dawes and Elmsley, he was shrewd and dexterous enough, but not, like Bentley and Porson, eminent. In literary comment he did not expatiate, although, or rather because, he was the most lettered scholar of his time. He stuck to business, as a scholar should, and preferred, as a man of letters will, the dry to the watery. He knew better than to conceive himself that rarest of all the great works of God, a literary critic; but such remarks on literature as he did let fall were very different stuff from the usual flummery of the cobbler who is ambitious to go beyond his last.

If his contemporaries rated him, both comparatively and absolutely, below his true position in the world of learning, the loss was chiefly theirs, but the blame was partly his. He had much of the boy in his composition, and something even of the schoolboy. His conversation in mixed company was apt to be flighty, and his writing, though it was not so, carried jauntiness of manner to some little excess. Those who judge weight by heaviness were perplexed and deceived by a colloquial gaiety, much less unseemly indeed than the frolic sallies of Dawes, but striking more sharply on the sense because not draped like them in the Latin toga; and it was disturbing to meet with a scholar who carried his levity, where others carry their gravity, on the surface, and was austere, where he might without offence or detection have been frivolous, in conducting the operations of his mind.

That he wrote little was the direct and natural consequence of his extraordinary capacity and the variety of his interests and attainments. He would rather improve himself than instruct others. He wrote on subjects where he could make definite and original contributions to the advancement of learning: otherwise he preferred to read.

Greek was his trade, but the home in which he dwelt was great literature, whether its language were Greek, Latin, English, French, Italian, Spanish, German, or Persian. The best authors were his study, but his reading ran far beyond them; his curiosity invaded holes and corners, and his taste ranged from the *Divine Comedy* to *Jorrocks's Jaunts*. He followed his inclinations and read for his own delight, with a keen and natural relish, not a dutiful and obedient admiration of the things which are admired by the wise and good. Nor were his studies warped and narrowed by ambition. A scholar who means to build himself a monument must spend much of his life in acquiring knowledge which for its own sake is not worth having and in reading books which do not in themselves deserve to be read; *at illa iacent multa et praeclara relicta.*

Music was a rival of literature in his affections, and his knowledge of the art and its history was almost an expert's. He followed with interest and understanding the progress of discovery in the natural sciences, and his acquaintance with zoology in particular was such as few laymen can boast. In conclusion it is proper to mention his vices. He was addicted to tobacco and indifferent to wine, and he would squander long summer days on watching the game of cricket.

His happy and useful life is over, and now begins the steady encroachment of oblivion, as those who remember him are in their turn summoned away. This record will not preserve, perhaps none could preserve, more than an indistinct and lifeless image of the friend who is lost to us: good, kind, bright, unselfish, and as honest as the day; versatile without shallowness, accomplished without ostentation, a treasury of hidden knowledge which only accident brought to light, but which accident brought to light perpetually, and which astonished us so often that astonishment lost its nature and we should have wondered more if wonders had failed. Yet what most eludes description is not the excellence of his gifts but the singularity of his essential being, his utter unlikeness to any other creature in the world.

VI

CEREMONIAL

I. THE TRINITY COLLEGE ADDRESSES

To the Reverend Henry Montagu Butler, D.D. (1913)[1]

I T would not be fitting that the completion of your eightieth year, an event which evokes congratulation from so many quarters, should be let pass without recognition and celebration by the society which for nearly twenty-seven years has known you as its Master. But ceremony and circumstance are ill suited to the close and domestic tie by which you are bound to those who now address you, and they have chosen the simplest fashion of expressing what they sincerely feel. They remember the distinction of your young life within these walls, your active services during the tenure of your fellowship, your prosperous labours and eminent success at Harrow, and, above all, the years of genial and dignified maturity during which you have presided over Trinity College; your ardent zeal for its common welfare, your considerate kindness towards its individual members, young and old, and the union of charm and authority with which you have represented it within the University and before the world; they recall the wisdom and tact with which you have fulfilled the duties of your office, and the prompt and graceful eloquence, issuing from rich stores of reading and memory, with which you have adorned it; and to their felicitations upon the just contentment which must on this anniversary be afforded you by the retrospect of your career, the happiness of your home, and the promise of your descendants, they add the assurance of their admiring and affectionate regard.

To Henry Jackson (1919)[2]

The present year, in which your eightieth birthday has been followed by your retirement from the office of Vice-Master, affords the Fellows of your College a suitable opportunity of expressing in symbol their affection for yourself and their sense of your services to the foundation which received you more than sixty years ago.

We therefore ask you to accept from us, as some token of these feelings, a copy of a vessel from which your most illustrious predecessor in the Chair of Greek is thought to have derived a solace not unknown or unwelcome to its present occupant; and we trust that the figure of Porson's tobacco-jar may often meet your eyes, and bring us before your mind, in moments tranquillised by its contents.

Our tribute carries with it the personal affection of friends and the gratitude of a community. From the day when first you were elected a Fellow of the College, no measure has been undertaken for the promotion of its welfare or the increase of its efficiency which has not been furthered by your zeal or due to your initiative. In Trinity, in Cambridge, in the whole academic world and far beyond it, you have earned a name on the lips of men and a place in their hearts to which few or none in the present or the past can make pretension. And this eminence you owe not only or chiefly to the fame of your learning and the influence of your teaching, nor even to that abounding and proverbial hospitality which for many a long year has made your rooms the hearthstone of the Society and a guesthouse in Cambridge for pilgrims from the ends of the earth, but to the broad and true humanity of your nature, endearing you alike to old and young, responsive to all varieties of character or pursuit, and remote from nothing that concerns mankind. The College which you have served and adorned so long, proud as it is of your intellect and attainments, and grateful for your devotion, is happy above all that in possessing you it possesses one of the great English worthies.

2. ADDRESS TO SIR JAMES GEORGE FRAZER
(1921)[3]

The friends and admirers who have united to found in your honour an annual lectureship in Social Anthropology, a science requiring no such link to connect it with your name, are not altogether content to set up their monument and withdraw in silence. They feel, and they hope that you will understand, the wish to approach more nearly an author whose works have bound to him in familiarity and affection even those to whom he is not personally known, and to indulge, by this short address, an emotion warmer than mere intellectual gratitude.

The Golden Bough, compared by Virgil to the mistletoe but now revealing some affinity to the banyan, has not only waxed a great tree but has spread to a spacious and hospitable forest, whose king receives homage in many tongues from a multitude resorting thither for its fruit or timber or refreshing shade. There they find learning mated with literature, labour disguised in ease, and a museum of dark and uncouth superstitions invested with the charm of a truly sympathetic magic. There you have gathered together, for the admonition of a proud and oblivious race, the scattered and fading relics of its foolish childhood, whether withdrawn from our view among savage folk and in distant countries, or lying unnoticed at our doors. The forgotten milestones of the road which man has travelled, the mazes and blind alleys of his appointed progress through time, are illuminated by your art and genius, and the strangest of remote and ancient things are brought near to the minds and hearts of your contemporaries.

They return you thanks for all that they have received at your hands, and they wish you years of life and continuance of strength to crown with new sheaves that rich and various harvest of discoveries which has already rewarded your untiring industry and your single-hearted quest of truth.

3. ADDRESS OF CONDOLENCE (1925)[4]

To the King's Most Excellent Majesty

May it please Your Majesty:

We, the Chancellor, Masters and Scholars of the University of Cambridge, beg leave humbly to approach Your Majesty with the assurance of our participation in the sorrow which has befallen the Royal House by the death of Your Majesty's august Mother, Queen Alexandra.

The sixty-two years which have gone by since the date when as an affianced bride She set foot upon these shores, and achieved in a day the second Danish conquest of England, more durable than the first, did but strengthen Her hold upon the affections which She had won, and build Her an ever surer home in the hearts of Her adopted people. Those inward and outward graces, that charm of bearing and address which was the visible effluence of a kind and gentle nature, that tender pity for suffering and misfortune, that prompt and overflowing generosity in their relief, will long be treasured in memory by the land which was privileged to know them; and their departure from earth, even in the fulness of years and the due course of nature, is yet mourned as premature. High and low, rich and poor, are united and drawn near to their Sovereign by a common sorrow at the loss of One beloved by all; and we, in loyal attachment to the Person and the Throne of Her Son, presume to lay at Your Majesty's feet the expression of our deep and reverent sympathy.

4. ADDRESS OF CONGRATULATION (1935)[5]

To the King's Most Excellent Majesty

May it please Your Majesty

We, the Chancellor, Masters, and Scholars of the University of Cambridge, desire to approach You with our loyal and dutiful congratulations on the completion of the twenty-fifth year of Your Majesty's reign.

The events of that reign, for greatness and moment, are such as have rarely been comprised within twenty-five years of human history. It has witnessed unexampled acceleration in the progress of man's acquaintance with the physical universe, his mastery of the forces of nature, and his skill in their application to the processes of industry and to the arts of life. No less to the contrivance of havoc and destruction has the advance of knowledge imparted new and prodigious efficacy; and it has been the lot of Your Majesty to confront at the head of your people the most formidable assault which has ever been delivered upon the safety and freedom of these realms. By exertion and sacrifice that danger was victoriously repelled; and Your Majesty's subjects, who have looked abroad upon the fall of states, the dissolution of systems, and a continent parcelled out anew, enjoy beneath your sceptre the retrospect of a period acquainted indeed with anxieties even within the body politic and perplexed by the emergence of new and difficult problems, but harmoniously combining stability with progress and rich in its contribution of benefits to the health and welfare of the community.

Not less than any portion of Your Majesty's kingdoms and empire has the University of Cambridge prospered in growth and development. New Statutes approved by Your Majesty in Council have organised its activities and enhanced its efficiency; the number of its students has increased, the range of its studies has widened, its resources have been augmented by noble benefactions; a city of new buildings provides accommodation for the vast extension and multiplication of the sciences, and eminent above all is the great fabric, lately opened by Your Majesty in person, which houses in spacious dignity the ancient library of our University and promises hospitality to the literature of centuries to come.

Nor was the University denied its part in the defence of Your Majesty's realm against the urgent peril which for more than four years encompassed it; and the time will long be remembered when our youth forsook their work and play to serve their King and country in battle, while their empty place was filled by other students and our courts and cloisters welcomed the invasion of soldiers undergoing instruction in the necessary arts of war. From the less novel pages of our domestic history we call to mind with especial pleasure the residence among us of two of Your Majesty's sons as members of our body and partners in our studies, confirming by the renewal of a personal tie the traditional attachment of the University to Your Majesty's illustrious house.

Called suddenly to the throne in an hour of vehement political contention, Your Majesty gave early evidence of the qualities which have since proved equal to every occasion. Courage and composure, steadfast impartiality, wise judgment and delicate feeling have ever been present and manifest; and a transparent openness of nature has knit Your Majesty to the affections of all your subjects, who, without respect of rank or condition, are conscious of what we may presume to call a fellow-feeling with their sovereign. That Your Majesty, with your august and beloved Consort at your side, may be granted long life and happy continuance of the blessings vouchsafed to your reign in the years already numbered is the earnest prayer of this University, even as it is the common hope of a people fortunate in their King and grateful for their fortune.

VII

THE NAME AND NATURE
OF POETRY

This lecture,[1] *the Leslie Stephen Lecture for 1933, was delivered at Cambridge on 9 May of that year.*

I T is my first duty to acknowledge the honour done me by those who have in their hands the appointment of the Leslie Stephen Lecturer, and to thank them for this token of their good will. My second duty is to say that I condemn their judgment and deplore their choice. It is twenty-two years to-day since I last, and first, spoke in this Senate-House; and in delivering my inaugural lecture, and telling this University what it was *not* to expect from me, I used these words.

Whether the faculty of literary criticism is the best gift that Heaven has in its treasuries I cannot say; but Heaven seems to think so, for assuredly it is the gift most charily bestowed. Orators and poets, sages and saints and heroes, if rare in comparison with blackberries, are commoner than returns of Halley's comet: literary critics are less common. And when, once in a century, or once in two centuries, the literary critic does appear—will some one in this home of mathematics tell me what are the chances that his appearance will be made among that small number of people who are called classical scholars? If this purely accidental conjunction occurred so lately as the eighteenth century in the person of Lessing, it ought to be a long while before it occurs again; and if so early a century as the twentieth is to witness it in another person, all I know is that I am not he.

In these twenty-two years I have improved in some respects and deteriorated in others; but I have not so much improved as to become a literary critic, nor so much deteriorated as to fancy that I have become one. Therefore you are not about to be addressed in that tone of authority which is appropriate to those who are, and is assumed by some of those who conceive themselves to be, literary critics. In order to hear Jehovah thundering out of Zion, or Little Bethel, you must go elsewhere.

But all my life long the best literature of several languages has been my favourite recreation; and good literature continually read for pleasure must, let us hope, do some good to the reader: must quicken his perception though dull, and sharpen his discrimination though blunt, and mellow the rawness of his personal opinions. But personal opinions they remain, not truths to be imparted as such with the sureness of superior insight and knowledge. I hope however that for brevity's sake, and your own, you will accept the disclaimer once for all, and that when hereafter I may say that things are thus or thus, you will not insist on my saying instead that I humbly venture to conceive them so or that I diffidently offer the suggestion to your better judgment.

There is indeed one literary subject on which I think I could discourse with profit, because it is also scientific, so that a man of science can handle it without presumption, and indeed is fitter for the task than most men of letters. The Artifice of Versification, which I first thought of taking for my theme today, has underlying it a set of facts which are unknown to most of those who practise it; and their success, when they succeed, is owing to instinctive tact and a natural goodness of ear. This latent base, comprising natural laws by which all versification is conditioned, and the secret springs of the pleasure which good versification can give, is little explored by critics: a few pages of Coventry Patmore and a few of Frederic

Myers contain all, so far as I know, or all of value, which
has been written on such matters;† and to these pages I
could add a few more. But they would not make a good
lecture: first, because of their fewness; secondly, because
of their dryness; and thirdly, because they might not be
easy for listeners to follow, and what I had to say would
be more clearly communicated by writing than by speech.
For these reasons I renounced my first intention, and chose
instead a subject much less precise, and therefore less
suitable to my capacity, and yet one which may be
treated, as I hope to treat it, with some degree of precision.

When one begins to discuss the nature of poetry, the
first impediment in the way is the inherent vagueness of
the name, and the number of its legitimate senses. It is
not bad English to speak of 'prose and poetry' in the sense
of 'prose and verse'. But it is wasteful; it squanders a
valuable word by stretching it to fit a meaning which is
accurately expressed by a wider term. Verse may be, like
'The Tale of Sir Thopas' in the judgment of Our Host of
the Tabard, 'rym dogerel'; and the name of poetry is
generally restricted to verse which can at least be called
literature, though it may differ from prose only in its
metrical form, and be superior to prose only in the superior

† I mean such matters as these: the existence in some metres, not in
others, of an inherent alternation of stresses, stronger and weaker; the
presence in verse of silent and invisible feet, like rests in music; the reason
why some lines of different length will combine harmoniously while others can
only be so combined by great skill or good luck; why, while blank verse can
be written in lines of ten or six syllables, a series of octosyllables ceases to
be verse if they are not rhymed; how Coleridge, in applying the new principle
which he announced in the preface to *Christabel*, has fallen between two
stools; the necessary limit to inversion of stress, which Milton understood
and Bridges overstepped; why, of two pairs of rhymes, equally correct and
both consisting of the same vowels and consonants, one is richer to the mental
ear and the other poorer; the office of alliteration in verse, and how its
definition must be narrowed if it is to be something which can perform
that office and not fail of its effect or actually defeat its purpose.

comeliness of that form itself, and the superior terseness which usually goes along with it. Then further there is verse which gives a positive and lively pleasure arising from the talent and accomplishment of its author.

> Now Gilpin had a pleasant wit
>   And loved a timely joke,
> And thus unto the Callender
>   In merry guise he spoke:
>
> I came because your horse would come;
>   And, if I well forbode,
> My hat and wig will soon be here:
>   They are upon the road.

Capital: but no one, if asked for a typical example of poetry, would recite those verses in reply. A typical example need not be any less plain and simple and straightforward, but it would be a little raised.

> Come, worthy Greek, Ulysses, come,
>   Possess these shores with me:
> The winds and seas are troublesome,
>   And here we may be free.
> Here may we sit and view their toil
>   That travail in the deep,
> And joy the day in mirth the while,
>   And spend the night in sleep.

There we are ceasing to gallop with the Callender's horse and beginning to fly with Pegasus. Indeed a promising young poetaster could not do better than lay up that stanza in his memory, not necessarily as a pattern to set before him, but as a touchstone to keep at his side. Diction and movement alike, it is perfect. It is made out of the most ordinary words, yet it is pure from the least alloy of prose; and however much nearer heaven the art of poetry may have mounted, it has never flown on a surer or a lighter wing.

It is perfect, I say; and nothing more than perfection can be demanded of anything: yet poetry is capable of more than this, and more therefore is expected from it. There is a conception of poetry which is not fulfilled by pure language and liquid versification, with the simple and so to speak colourless pleasure which they afford, but involves the presence in them of something which moves and touches in a special and recognisable way. Set beside that stanza of Daniel's these lines from Bruce's or Logan's 'Cuckoo':

> Sweet bird, thy bower is ever green,
>   Thy sky is ever clear;
> Thou hast no sorrow in thy song,
>   No winter in thy year.

There a new element has stolen in, a tinge of emotion. And I think that to transfuse emotion—not to transmit thought but to set up in the reader's sense a vibration corresponding to what was felt by the writer—is the peculiar function of poetry. Even where the verse is not thus beautiful and engaging in its external form, as in Johnson's lines,

> His virtues walked their narrow round,
>   Nor made a pause, nor left a void;
> And sure the Eternal Master found
>   The single talent well employed,

it may yet possess the same virtue and elicit a like response.

Further than this I will not now ascend the stair of poetry. I have chosen these two examples because they may almost be called humble, and contain hardly more than the promise of what poetry attains to be. Here it is not lofty or magnificent or intense; it does not transport with rapture nor overwhelm with awe; it does not stab the heart nor shake the soul nor take the breath away. But it is poetry, though not in the highest, yet in the highest definable sense.

> Duncan is in his grave;
> After life's fitful fever he sleeps well.

Even for that poetry there is no other name.

I said that the legitimate meanings of the word poetry were themselves so many as to embarrass the discussion of its nature. All the more reason why we should not confound confusion worse by wresting the term to licentious use and affixing it either to dissimilar things already provided with names of their own, or to new things for which new names should be invented.

There was a whole age of English in which the place of poetry was usurped by something very different which possessed the proper and specific name of wit: wit not in its modern sense, but as defined by Johnson, 'a combination of dissimilar images, or discovery of occult resemblances in things apparently unlike'. Such discoveries are no more poetical than anagrams; such pleasure as they give is purely intellectual and is intellectually frivolous; but this was the pleasure principally sought and found in poems by the intelligentsia of fifty years and more of the seventeenth century. Some of the writers who purveyed it to their contemporaries were, by accident, considerable poets; and though their verse was generally inharmonious, and apparently cut into lengths and tied into faggots by deaf mathematicians, some little of their poetry was beautiful and even superb. But it was not by this that they captivated and sought to captivate. Simile and metaphor, things inessential to poetry, were their great engrossing preoccupation, and were prized the more in proportion as they were further fetched. They did not mean these accessories to be helpful, to make their sense clearer or their conceptions more vivid; they hardly even meant them for ornament, or cared whether an image had any independent power to please: their object was to startle by novelty and amuse by ingenuity a public whose one wish was to be so startled and amused. The pleasure, however luxurious, of hearing St Mary Magdalene's eyes described as

> Two walking baths, two weeping motions,
> Portable and compendious oceans,

was not a poetic pleasure; and poetry, as a label for this
particular commodity, is not appropriate.

Appropriateness is even more carefully to be considered
when the thing which we so much admire that we wish
to give it the noblest name we can lay our tongue to is a
new thing. We should beware of treating the word poetry
as chemists have treated the word salt. Salt is a crystalline
substance recognised by its taste; its name is as old as the
English language and is the possession of the English people,
who know what it means: it is not the private property
of a science less than three hundred years old, which,
being in want of a term to embody a new conception, 'an
acid having the whole or part of its hydrogen replaced by
a metal', has lazily helped itself to the old and unsuitable
word salt, instead of excogitating a new and therefore to
that extent an apt one. The right model for imitation is
that chemist who, when he encountered, or thought he had
encountered, a hitherto nameless form of matter, did not
purloin for it the name of something else, but invented out
of his own head a name which should be proper to it, and
enriched the vocabulary of modern man with the useful
word *gas*. If we apply the word poetry to an object which
does not resemble, either in form or content, anything
which has heretofore been so called, not only are we mal-
treating and corrupting language, but we may be guilty
of disrespect and blasphemy. Poetry may be too mean a
name for the object in question: the object, being certainly
something different, may possibly be something superior.
When the Lord rained bread from heaven so that man did
eat angels' food, and the children of Israel saw upon the
face of the wilderness a small round thing, as small as
the hoar frost on the ground, they did not call it quails:

they rose to the occasion and said to one another 'it is manna'.

There is also such a thing as sham poetry, a counterfeit deliberately manufactured and offered as a substitute. In English the great historical example is certain verse produced abundantly and applauded by high and low in what for literary purposes is loosely called the eighteenth century: not a hundred years accidentally begun and ended by chronology, but a longer period which is a unity and a reality; the period lying between 'Samson Agonistes' in 1671 and the *Lyrical Ballads* in 1798, and including as an integral part and indeed as its most potent influence the mature work of Dryden.

Matthew Arnold more than fifty years ago, in speaking of Wordsworth's and Coleridge's low estimate of the poetry of the eighteenth century, issued the warning 'there are many signs to show that the eighteenth century and its judgments are coming into favour again'. I remember thinking to myself that surely this could never be; but there you see what it is to be a literary critic. There has now for a good many years been a strong disposition to revise the verdict pronounced by the nineteenth century on the poetry of the eighteenth and to represent that its disparaging judgment was no more than an expression of distaste for a sort of poetry unlike its own. That is a misconception. It set a low value on the poetry of the eighteenth century, not because it differed in kind from its own, but because, even at its best, it differed in quality, as its own best poetry did not differ, from the poetry of all those ages, whether modern or ancient, English or foreign, which are acknowledged as the great ages of poetry. Tried by that standard the poetry of the eighteenth century, even when not vicious, even when sound and good, fell short.

The literature of the eighteenth century in England is an admirable and most enjoyable thing. It has a greater solidity of excellence than any before or after; and although the special task and characteristic achievement of the age was the invention and establishment of a healthy, work-manlike, athletic prose, to supersede the cumbrous and decorated and self-admiring prose of a Milton or a Jeremy Taylor, and to become a trustworthy implement for accurate thinking and the serious pursuit of truth, yet in verse also it created masterpieces, and perhaps no English poem of greater than lyric length, not even 'The Nonne's Priest's Tale' or 'The Ancient Mariner', is quite so perfect as 'The Rape of the Lock'. But the human faculty which dominated the eighteenth century and informed its literature was the intelligence, and that involved, as Arnold says, 'some repressing and silencing of poetry', 'some touch of frost to the imaginative life of the soul'. Man had ceased to live from the depths of his nature; he occupied himself for choice with thoughts which do not range beyond the sphere of the understanding; he lighted the candles and drew down the blind to shut out that patroness of poets, the moon. The writing of poetry proceeded, and much of the poetry written was excellent literature; but excellent literature which is also poetry is not therefore excellent poetry, and the poetry of the eighteenth century was most satisfactory when it did not try to be poetical. Eighteenth-century poetry is in fact a name for two different things, which ought to be kept distinct. There was a good sound workaday article, efficiently discharging a worthy and honourable though not an exalted duty. Satire, controversy, and burlesque, to which the eighteenth century was drawn by the character of its genius, and in which its achievement was unrivalled, are forms of art in which high poetry is not at home, and to which, unless introduced with great parsimony and tact, it would be actually injurious and disfiguring. The conclusion of *The Dunciad* may fairly be called sublime; but such a tone was wisely reserved for the conclusion. The modicum of the poetical element which satire can easily accommodate is rather what we find in lines like these:

> Riches, like insects, when conceal'd they lie,
> Wait but for wings, and in their season fly.
> Who sees pale Mammon pine amidst his store
> Sees but a backward steward for the poor:
> This year a reservoir, to keep and spare;
> The next, a fountain, spouting through his heir,
> In lavish streams to quench a country's thirst,
> And men and dogs shall drink him till they burst.

And what sterling stuff they are! But such writing, which was their true glory and should have been their proper pride, did not content its writers. They felt that this, after all, did not rank as equal with the poetry of other ages, nor fulfil the conception of poetry which was obscurely present in their minds; and they aspired to something which should be less pedestrian. It was as though the ostrich should attempt to fly. The ostrich on her own element is the swiftest of created things; she scorneth the horse and his rider; and although we are also told that God hath deprived her of wisdom, neither hath he imparted to her understanding, he has at any rate given her sense enough to know that she is not a lark or an eagle. To poets of the eighteenth century high and impassioned poetry did not come spontaneously, because the feelings which foster its birth were not then abundant and urgent in the inner man; but they girt up their loins and essayed a lofty strain at the bidding of ambition. The way to write real poetry, they thought, must be to write something as little like prose as possible; they devised for the purpose what was called a 'correct and splendid diction', which consisted in always using the wrong word instead of the right, and plastered it as ornament, with no thought of propriety, on whatever they desired to dignify. It commanded notice and was not easy to mistake; so the public mind soon connected it with the notion of poetry and came in course of time to regard it as alone poetical.†

It was in truth at once pompous and poverty-stricken. It had a very limited, because supposedly choice, vocabulary, and was consequently unequal to the multitude and refinement of its duties. It could not describe natural objects with sensitive fidelity to nature; it could not express human feelings with a variety and delicacy answering to their own. A thick, stiff, unaccommodating medium was interposed between the writer and his work. And this deadening of language had a consequence beyond its own sphere: its effect worked inward, and deadened perception. That which could no longer be described was no longer noticed.

† It is now customary to say that the nineteenth century had a similar lingo of its own. A lingo it had, or came to have, and in the seventies and eighties the minor poets and poetasters were all using the same supposedly poetic diction. It was imitative and sapless, but not preposterous: its leading characteristic was a stale and faded prettiness.

> As one that for a weary space has lain
>   Lull'd by the song of Circe and her wine
>   In gardens near the pale of Proserpine,
> Where that Æean isle forgets the main,
> And only the low lutes of love complain,
>   And only shadows of wan lovers pine—
>   As such an one were glad to know the brine
> Salt on his lips, and the large air again....

The atmosphere of the eighteenth century made much better poets write much worse.

> Lo! where the rosy-bosom'd Hours,
>   Fair Venus' train, appear,
> Disclose the long-expecting flowers
>   And wake the purple year!
> The Attic warbler pours her throat

and so forth.

The features and formation of the style can be studied under a cruel light in Dryden's translations from Chaucer. The Knight's 'Tale of Palamon and Arcite' is not one of Chaucer's most characteristic and successful poems: he is not perfectly at home, as in the 'Prologue' and the 'Tale of Chauntecleer and Pertelote', and his movement is a trifle languid. Dryden's translation shows Dryden in the maturity of his power and accomplishment, and much of it can be honestly and soberly admired. Nor was he insensible to all the peculiar excellence of Chaucer: he had the wit to keep unchanged such lines as 'Up rose the sun and up rose Emily' or 'The slayer of himself yet saw I there'; he understood that neither he nor anyone else could better them. But much too often in a like case he would try to improve, because he thought that he could. He believed, as he says himself, that he was 'turning some of *The Canterbury Tales* into our language, as it is now refined'; 'the words' he says again 'are given up as a post not to be defended in our poet, because he wanted the modern art of fortifying'; 'in some places' he tells us 'I have added somewhat of my own where I thought my author was deficient, and had not given his thoughts their true lustre, for want of words in the beginning of our language'.

Let us look at the consequences. Chaucer's vivid and memorable line

> The smiler with the knife under the cloke

becomes these three:

> Next stood Hypocrisy, with holy leer,
> Soft smiling and demurely looking down,
> But hid the dagger underneath the gown.

Again:

> Alas, quod he, that day that I was bore.

So Chaucer, for want of words in the beginning of our language. Dryden comes to his assistance and gives his thoughts their true lustre thus:

> Cursed be the day when first I did appear;
> Let it be blotted from the calendar.
> Lest it pollute the month and poison all the year.

Or yet again:

> The queen anon for very womanhead
> Gan for to weep, and so did Emily
> And all the ladies in the company.

If Homer or Dante had the same thing to say, would he wish to say it otherwise? But to Dryden Chaucer wanted the modern art of fortifying, which he thus applies:

> He said; dumb sorrow seized the standers-by.
> The queen, above the rest, by nature good
> (The pattern formed of perfect womanhood)
> For tender pity wept: when she began
> Through the bright quire the infectious virtue ran.
> All dropped their tears, even the contended maid.

Had there not fallen upon England the curse out of Isaiah, 'make the heart of this people fat, and make their ears heavy, and shut their eyes'? That there should ever have existed an obtuseness which could mistake this impure verbiage for a correct and splendid diction is a dreadful thought. More dreadful is the experience of seeing it poured profusely, continually, and with evident exultation, from the pen of a great and deservedly illustrious author. But most dreadful of all is the reflexion that he was himself its principal origin. The correctness of calling Emily 'the contended maid' is his correctness, and the splendour of 'through the bright quire the infectious virtue ran' is his own infectious vice. His disciple Pope admired this line so much that he put it twice into his *Iliad*.

> Through all her train the soft infection ran.
>
> The infectious softness through the heroes ran.

This same Dryden, when his self-corrupted taste and the false guidance of ambition would let him, could write in verse even better than he wrote in prose, dipping his bucket in the same well of pure, wholesome, racy English. What a joy it is to whistle correctness and splendour down the wind, and hear him speak out straight in the vernacular.

> Till frowning skies began to change their cheer,
> And time turned up the wrong side of the year.
>
> Bare benting times and moulting months may come,
> When lagging late they cannot reach their home.
>
> Your benefices twinkled from afar;
> They found the new Messiah by the star.

And not only in his domestic sphere of satire and controversy but in this very book of *Fables*, where he is venturing abroad. To his translation of 'The Flower and the Leaf' he prefixed these nineteen lines of his own.

> Now, turning from the wintry signs, the Sun
> His course exalted through the Ram had run,
> And whirling up the skies his chariot drove
> Through Taurus and the lightsome realms of Love,
> Where Venus from her orb descends in showers
> To glad the ground and paint the fields with flowers:
> When first the tender blades of grass appear
> And buds that yet the blast of Eurus fear
> Stand at the door of life and doubt to clothe the year,
> Till gentle heat and soft repeated rains
> Make the green blood to dance within their veins.
> Then at their call emboldened out they come
> And swell the gems and burst the narrow room,
> Broader and broader yet their blooms display,
> Salute the welcome sun and entertain the day.

> Then from their breathing souls the sweets repair
> To scent the skies and purge the unwholesome air:
> Joy spreads the heart, and with a general song
> Spring issues out and leads the jolly months along.

What exuberant beauty and vigour! and what nature!
I believe that I admire that passage more heartily and
relish it more keenly than Pope or Johnson or Dryden's
own contemporaries could, because I live outside their
dungeon, the dungeon in which Dryden himself had shut
them up; because my ears are not contentedly attuned to
the choir of captives singing hymns in the prison chapel,
but can listen to the wild music that burdens every bough
in the free world outside the wall.

Not that even this passage will quite sustain that comparison. When I am drinking Barolo stravecchio in Turin,
I am not disturbed, nor even visited, by the reflexion that
there is better wine in Dijon. But yet there is; and there
was better poetry, not reckoning Milton's, even in the
perverse and crooked generation preceding Dryden.
Thinly scattered on that huge dross-heap, the Caroline
Parnassus, there were tiny gems of purer ray; and the most
genuine of Dryden's own poetry is to be found, never
more than four lines at once, seldom more than two, in
his early, unshapely, and wearisome poem the *Annus
Mirabilis*.

His great successor, whose *Iliad* was a more dazzling
and seductive example of the false manner than any work
of Dryden's own, and became, as Coleridge said, 'the
main source of our pseudo-poetic diction'—Pope, though
he threw open to others the wide gate, did not long keep
them company on the broad way, which led them to
destruction. He came to recognise, and for the last twenty
years of his life he steadily followed, the true bent of his
genius, in satire or disputation: into these he put no larger

quantity and no rarer quality of poetry than they would assimilate, and he made no more ascents in the balloon. Pope had less of the poetic gift than Dryden; in common with his contemporaries he drew from a poorer vocabulary; and his versification, though more evenly good, did not reach the buoyant excellence of Dryden's at its best. What lifts him nearest to true poetry is sincere inward ardour. Pope had a soul in his body, an aery and fiery particle, where Dryden had nothing but a lump of clay, and he can be nobler than Dryden can. But not even in the elegy 'To the memory of an unfortunate lady' does the fire burn clear of smoke, and truth of emotion do itself full justice in naturalness and purity of diction.

Nuns fret not at their convent's narrow room, and the eighteenth century, except for a few malcontents, was satisfied with what its leading poets provided. 'It is surely superfluous' says Johnson 'to answer the question that has once been asked, whether Pope was a poet, otherwise than by asking in return, if Pope be not a poet, where is poetry to be found?' It is to be found, Dr Johnson, in Dr Watts.

> Soft and easy is thy cradle;
>   Coarse and hard thy Saviour lay,
> When his birthplace was a stable
>   And his softest bed was hay.

That simple verse, bad rhyme and all, is poetry beyond Pope. It is to be found again, Samuel, in your namesake Benjamin, as tough a piece of timber as yourself.

> What gentle ghost, besprent with April dew,
> Hails me so solemnly to yonder yew,
> And beckoning woos me, from the fatal tree,
> To pluck a garland for herself or me?

When Pope imitated that, he got no nearer than this:

> What beck'ning ghost along the moon-light shade
> Invites my steps and points to yonder glade?
> 'Tis she!—but why that bleeding bosom gor'd, etc.

When I hear anyone say, with defiant emphasis, that Pope was a poet, I suspect him of calling in ambiguity of language to promote confusion of thought. That Pope was a poet is true; but it is one of those truths which are beloved of liars, because they serve so well the cause of falsehood. That Pope was not a poet is false; but a righteous man, standing in awe of the last judgment and the lake which burneth with fire and brimstone, might well prefer to say it.

It is impossible to admire such poetry as Pope's so whole-heartedly as Johnson did, and to rest in it with such perfect contentment, without losing the power to appreciate finer poetry or even to recognise it when met. Johnson's unlucky frankness in letting the world know how he was affected by 'Lycidas' has earned his critical judgment discredit enough; but consider also his response to poetry which, though somehow written in the eighteenth century, is of an alien strain and worthy of other ages; consider his attitude to Collins. For Collins himself he felt esteem and liking, and his kind heart must have made him wish to speak well of his friend's poetry; but he was an honest man, and could not.

The first impediment, I said, to dealing with the subject of poetry is the native ambiguity of the term. But the course of these remarks has now brought us to a point where another and perhaps greater difficulty awaits us in determining the competence or incompetence of the judge, that is the sensibility or insensibility of the percipient. Am I capable of recognising poetry if I come across it? Do I possess the organ by which poetry is perceived? The majority of civilised mankind notoriously and indisputably do not; who has certified me that I am one of the minority who do? I may know what I like and admire, I may like and admire it intensely; but what makes me think that it is poetry? Is my reason for thinking so anything more than this: that poetry is generally esteemed the highest form of literature, and that my opinion of myself forbids me to believe that what I most like and admire is anything short of the highest? Yet why be unwilling to admit that perhaps you cannot perceive poetry? Why think it necessary to your self-respect that you should? How many of the good and great, how many saints and heroes have possessed this faculty? Can you hear the shriek of the bat? Probably not; but do you think the less of yourself on that account? do you pretend to others, or even try to persuade yourself, that you can? Is it an unbearable thing, and crushing to self-conceit, to be in the majority?

If a man is insensible to poetry, it does not follow that he gets no pleasure from poems. Poems very seldom consist of poetry and nothing else; and pleasure can be derived also from their other ingredients. I am convinced that most readers, when they think that they are admiring poetry, are deceived by inability to analyse their sensations, and that they are really admiring, not the poetry of the passage before them, but something else in it, which they like better than poetry.

To begin with a very obvious instance. I have been told by devout women that to them the most beautiful poetry is Keble's. Keble is a poet; there are things in *The Christian Year* which can be admired by atheists; but what devout women most prize in it, as Keble himself would have wished, is not its poetry; and I much doubt whether any of them, if asked to pick out the best poem in the book, would turn at once to the Second Sunday after Easter. Good religious poetry, whether in Keble or Dante or Job, is likely to be most justly appreciated and most discriminatingly relished by the undevout.

Again, there existed in the last century a great body of

Wordsworthians, as they were called. It is now much smaller; but true appreciation of Wordsworth's poetry has not diminished in proportion: I suspect that it has much increased. The Wordsworthians, as Matthew Arnold told them, were apt to praise their poet for the wrong things. They were most attracted by what may be called his philosophy; they accepted his belief in the morality of the universe and the tendency of events to good; they were even willing to entertain his conception of nature as a living and sentient and benignant being, a conception as purely mythological as the Dryads and the Naiads. To that thrilling utterance which pierces the heart and brings tears to the eyes of thousands who care nothing for his opinions and beliefs they were not noticeably sensitive; and however justly they admired the depth of his insight into human nature and the nobility of his moral ideas, these things, with which his poetry was in close and harmonious alliance, are distinct from poetry itself.

When I examine my mind and try to discern clearly in the matter, I cannot satisfy myself that there are any such things as poetical ideas. No truth, it seems to me, is too precious, no observation too profound, and no sentiment too exalted to be expressed in prose. The utmost that I could admit is that some ideas do, while others do not, lend themselves kindly to poetical expression; and that these receive from poetry an enhancement which glorifies and almost transfigures them, and which is not perceived to be a separate thing except by analysis.

'Whosoever will save his life shall lose it, and whosoever will lose his life shall find it.' That is the most important truth which has ever been uttered, and the greatest discovery ever made in the moral world; but I do not find in it anything which I should call poetical. On the other hand, when Wisdom says in the Proverbs 'He that sinneth against me wrongeth his own soul; all they that hate me, love death', that is to me poetry, because of the words in which the idea is clothed; and as for the seventh verse of the forty-ninth Psalm in the Book of Common Prayer, 'But no man may deliver his brother, nor make agreement unto God for him', that is to me poetry so moving that I can hardly keep my voice steady in reading it. And that this is the effect of language I can ascertain by experiment: the same thought in the bible version, 'None of them can by any means redeem his brother, nor give to God a ransom for him', I can read without emotion.

Poetry is not the thing said but a way of saying it. Can it then be isolated and studied by itself? for the combination of language with its intellectual content, its meaning, is as close a union as can well be imagined. Is there such a thing as pure unmingled poetry, poetry independent of meaning?

Even when poetry has a meaning, as it usually has, it may be inadvisable to draw it out. 'Poetry gives most pleasure' said Coleridge 'when only generally and not perfectly understood'; and perfect understanding will sometimes almost extinguish pleasure. 'The Haunted Palace' is one of Poe's best poems so long as we are content to swim in the sensations it evokes and only vaguely to apprehend the allegory. We are roused to discomfort, at least I am, when we begin to perceive how exact in detail the allegory is; when it dawns upon us that the fair palace door is Roderick Usher's mouth, the pearl and ruby his teeth and lips, the yellow banners his hair, the ramparts plumed and pallid his forehead, and when we are reduced to hoping, for it is no more than a hope, that the wingèd odours have no connexion with hair-oil.

Meaning is of the intellect, poetry is not. If it were, the eighteenth century would have been able to write it better. As matters actually stand, who are the English poets of that age in whom pre-eminently one can hear and recognise the true poetic accent emerging clearly from the contemporary dialect? These four: Collins, Christopher Smart, Cowper, and Blake. And what other characteristic had these four in common? They were mad. Remember Plato: 'He who without the Muses' madness in his soul comes knocking at the door of poesy and thinks that art will make him anything fit to be called a poet, finds that the poetry which he indites in his sober senses is beaten hollow by the poetry of madmen.'

That the intellect is not the fount of poetry, that it may actually hinder its production, and that it cannot even be trusted to recognise poetry when produced, is best seen in the case of Smart. Neither the prize founded in this University by the Rev. Thomas Seaton nor the successive contemplation of five several attributes of the Supreme Being could incite him to good poetry while he was sane. The only poem by which he is remembered, a poem which came to its own in the kinder climate of the nineteenth century and has inspired one of the best poems of the twentieth, was written, if not, as tradition says, in actual confinement, at any rate very soon after release; and when the eighteenth century, the age of sanity and intelligence, collected his poetical works, it excluded this piece as 'bearing melancholy proofs of the recent estrangement of his mind'.

Collins and Cowper, though they saw the inside of mad-houses, are not supposed to have written any of their poetry there; and Blake was never mad enough to be locked up. But elements of their nature were more or less insurgent against the centralised tyranny of the intellect, and their brains were not thrones on which the great usurper could sit secure. And so it strangely came to pass that in the eighteenth century, the age of prose and of unsound or unsatisfying poetry, there sprang up one well of the purest inspiration. For me the most poetical of all poets is Blake. I find his lyrical note as beautiful as Shakespeare's and more beautiful than anyone else's; and I call him more poetical than Shakespeare, even though Shakespeare has so much more poetry, because poetry in him preponderates more than in Shakespeare over everything else, and instead of being confounded in a great river can be drunk pure from a slender channel of its own. Shakespeare is rich in thought, and his meaning has power of itself to move us, even if the poetry were not there: Blake's meaning is often unimportant or virtually non-existent, so that we can listen with all our hearing to his celestial tune.

Even Shakespeare, who had so much to say, would sometimes pour out his loveliest poetry in saying nothing.

> Take O take those lips away
>   That so sweetly were forsworn,
> And those eyes, the break of day,
>   Lights that do mislead the morn;
> But my kisses bring again,
>   bring again,
> Seals of love, but seal'd in vain,
>   seal'd in vain.

That is nonsense; but it is ravishing poetry. When Shakespeare fills such poetry with thought, and thought which is worthy of it, as in 'Fear no more the heat o' the sun' or 'O mistress mine, where are you roaming?' those songs, the very summits of lyrical achievement, are indeed greater and more moving poems, but I hardly know how to call them more poetical.

Now Blake again and again, as Shakespeare now and then, gives us poetry neat, or adulterated with so little meaning that nothing except poetical emotion is perceived and matters.

> Hear the voice of the Bard,
>   Who present, past, and future sees;
> Whose ears have heard
> The Holy Word
>   That walk'd among the ancient trees.
>
> Calling the lapsèd soul
>   And weeping in the evening dew;
> That might control
> The starry pole,
>   And fallen, fallen light renew.
>
> 'O Earth, O Earth, return!
>   Arise from out the dewy grass;
> Night is worn,
> And the morn
>   Rises from the slumberous mass.
>
> 'Turn away no more;
>   Why wilt thou turn away?
> The starry floor,
> The watery shore
>   Is giv'n thee till the break of day.'

That mysterious grandeur would be less grand if it were
less mysterious; if the embryo ideas which are all that it
contains should endue form and outline, and suggestion
condense itself into thought.

> Memory, hither come
>   And tune your merry notes;
> And while upon the wind
>   Your music floats
> I'll pore upon the stream
> Where sighing lovers dream,
> And fish for fancies as they pass
> Within the watery glass.

That answers to nothing real; memory's merry notes and
the rest are empty phrases, not things to be imagined;
the stanza does but entangle the reader in a net of thoughtless delight. The verses which I am now going to read
probably possessed for Blake a meaning, and his students

think that they have found it; but the meaning is a poor
foolish disappointing thing in comparison with the verses
themselves.

> My Spectre around me night and day
> Like a wild beast guards my way;
> My Emanation far within
> Weeps incessantly for my sin.
>
> A fathomless and boundless deep,
> There we wander, there we weep;
> On the hungry craving wind
> My Spectre follows thee behind.
>
> He scents thy footsteps in the snow
> Wheresoever thou dost go:
> Through the wintry hail and rain
> When wilt thou return again?
>
> Dost thou not in pride and scorn
> Fill with tempests all my morn,
> And with jealousies and fears
> Fill my pleasant nights with tears?
>
> Seven of my sweet loves thy knife
> Has bereavèd of their life.
> Their marble tombs I built with tears
> And with cold and shuddering fears.
>
> Seven more loves weep night and day
> Round the tombs where my loves lay,
> And seven more loves attend each night
> Around my couch with torches bright.
>
> And seven more loves in my bed
> Crown with wine my mournful head,
> Pitying and forgiving all
> Thy transgressions great and small.
>
> When wilt thou return and view
> My loves, and them to life renew?
> When wilt thou return and live?
> When wilt thou pity as I forgive?

I am not equal to framing definite ideas which would match
that magnificent versification and correspond to the strong
tremor of unreasonable excitement which those words set

up in some region deeper than the mind. Lastly take this stanza, addressed 'to the Accuser who is the God of this World'.

> Tho' thou art worship'd by the names divine
> Of Jesus and Jehovah, thou art still
> The Son of Morn in weary Night's decline,
> The lost traveller's dream under the hill.

It purports to be theology: what theological sense, if any, it may have, I cannot imagine and feel no wish to learn: it is pure and self-existent poetry, which leaves no room in me for anything besides.

In most poets, as I said, poetry is less often found thus disengaged from its usual concomitants, from certain things with which it naturally unites itself and seems to blend indistinguishably. For instance:

> Sorrow, that is not sorrow, but delight;
> And miserable love, that is not pain
> To hear of, for the glory that redounds
> Therefrom to human kind, and what we are.

The feeling with which those lines are read is composite, for one constituent is supplied by the depth and penetrating truth of the thought. Again:

> Though love repine and reason chafe,
>   There came a voice without reply,—
> ''Tis man's perdition to be safe,
>   When for the truth he ought to die'.

Much of the emotion kindled by that verse can be referred to the nobility of the sentiment. But in these six simple words of Milton—

> Nymphs and shepherds, dance no more—

what is it that can draw tears, as I know it can, to the eyes of more readers than one? What in the world is there to cry about? Why have the mere words the physical effect of pathos when the sense of the passage is blithe and gay? I can only say, because they are poetry, and find their way to something in man which is obscure and latent, something older than the present organisation of his nature, like the patches of fen which still linger here and there in the drained lands of Cambridgeshire.

Poetry indeed seems to me more physical than intellectual. A year or two ago, in common with others, I received from America a request that I would define poetry. I replied that I could no more define poetry than a terrier can define a rat, but that I thought we both recognised the object by the symptoms which it provokes in us. One of these symptoms was described in connexion with another object by Eliphaz the Temanite: 'A spirit passed before my face: the hair of my flesh stood up.' Experience has taught me, when I am shaving of a morning, to keep watch over my thoughts, because, if a line of poetry strays into my memory, my skin bristles so that the razor ceases to act. This particular symptom is accompanied by a shiver down the spine; there is another which consists in a constriction of the throat and a precipitation of water to the eyes; and there is a third which I can only describe by borrowing a phrase from one of Keats's last letters, where he says, speaking of Fanny Brawne, 'everything that reminds me of her goes through me like a spear'. The seat of this sensation is the pit of the stomach.

My opinions on poetry are necessarily tinged, perhaps I should say tainted, by the circumstance that I have come into contact with it on two sides. We were saying a while ago that poetry is a very wide term, and inconveniently comprehensive: so comprehensive is it that it embraces two books, fortunately not large ones, of my own. I know how this stuff came into existence; and though I have no right to assume that any other poetry came into existence in the same way, yet I find reason to believe that some

poetry, and quite good poetry, did. Wordsworth for
instance says that poetry is the spontaneous overflow of
powerful feelings, and Burns has left us this confession,
'I have two or three times in my life composed from the
wish rather than the impulse, but I never succeeded to
any purpose'. In short I think that the production of
poetry, in its first stage, is less an active than a passive and
involuntary process; and if I were obliged, not to define
poetry, but to name the class of things to which it belongs,
I should call it a secretion; whether a natural secretion,
like turpentine in the fir, or a morbid secretion, like the
pearl in the oyster. I think that my own case, though I may
not deal with the material so cleverly as the oyster does,
is the latter; because I have seldom written poetry unless
I was rather out of health, and the experience, though
pleasurable, was generally agitating and exhausting. If
only that you may know what to avoid, I will give some
account of the process.

Having drunk a pint of beer at luncheon—beer is a
sedative to the brain, and my afternoons are the least
intellectual portion of my life—I would go out for a walk
of two or three hours. As I went along, thinking of nothing
in particular, only looking at things around me and following the progress of the seasons, there would flow into my
mind, with sudden and unaccountable emotion, sometimes
a line or two of verse, sometimes a whole stanza at once,
accompanied, not preceded, by a vague notion of the
poem which they were destined to form part of. Then
there would usually be a lull of an hour or so, then perhaps
the spring would bubble up again. I say bubble up,
because, so far as I could make out, the source of the sug-
gestions thus proffered to the brain was an abyss which
I have already had occasion to mention, the pit of the
stomach. When I got home I wrote them down, leaving

gaps, and hoping that further inspiration might be forth-coming another day. Sometimes it was, if I took my walks in a receptive and expectant frame of mind; but some-times the poem had to be taken in hand and completed by the brain, which was apt to be a matter of trouble and anxiety, involving trial and disappointment, and some-times ending in failure. I happen to remember distinctly the genesis of the piece which stands last in my first volume. Two of the stanzas, I do not say which, came into my head, just as they are printed, while I was crossing the corner of Hampstead Heath between the Spaniard's Inn and the footpath to Temple Fortune. A third stanza came with a little coaxing after tea. One more was needed, but it did not come: I had to turn to and compose it myself, and that was a laborious business. I wrote it thirteen times, and it was more than a twelvemonth before I got it right.

By this time you must be sated with anatomy, pathology, and autobiography, and willing to let me retire from my incursion into the foreign territory of literary criticism. Farewell for ever. I will not say with Coleridge that I recentre my immortal mind in the deep sabbath of meek self-content; but I shall go back with relief and thankful-ness to my proper job.

APPENDIX

The following paragraphs are all that survive of a paper of the 1890's on Matthew Arnold.[1]

On the last day of October 1891 a bust of Matthew Arnold was unveiled in Westminster Abbey by his friend and contemporary Lord Coleridge. Lord Coleridge on that occasion delivered an address in which, by way of conveying to his audience a clear conception of what Matthew Arnold was, he explained to them with great particularity what Matthew Arnold was not. 'Thackeray' said he 'may have written more pungent social satire, Tennyson may be a greater poet, John Morley may be a greater critical biographer, Cardinal Newman may have a more splendid style, Lightfoot or Ellicott or Jowett may be greater ecclesiastical scholars and have done more for the interpretation of St Paul.' Here the list ends: I cannot imagine why; for it appears to me that if I were once started I could go on like that for ever. Mr Chevalier may be a more accomplished vocalist, Mr Gladstone may be an older Parliamentary hand, Mr Stoddart may have made higher scores against the Australians, the Lord Chief Justice may have sentenced a greater number of criminals to penal servitude—where is one to stop? all these personages have as much business here as that great biographer Mr John Morley. And as for the superb constellation of divines,—Lightfoot and Ellicott and Jowett,—what I want to know is, where is Archdeacon Farrar? But if, after all, Lord Coleridge's account of what Arnold was not, leaves it still a trifle vague what Arnold was, let me take you to the *Daily Chronicle* of April 17, 1888. I copied down its remarks that same day; and ever since, I carry them about with me wherever I go as a sort of intellectual salvolatile. Whenever I am in any ways afflicted or distressed in mind, body or estate, I take out this extract and read it; and then, like the poet Longfellow when he gazed on the planet Mars, I am strong again. The following are the salient characteristics of Matthew Arnold's poetry—'His muse mounted upward with bright thoughts, as the skylark shakes dewdrops from its wing as it carols at "Heaven's Gate," or, like a mountain brooklet carrying many a wild flower on its wavelets, his melody flowed cheerily on. Sometimes too his music rises like that of the mysterious ocean casting up pearls as it rolls.'

Now at last I hope you have a clear conception of the real Matthew Arnold: now you will be able to recognise his poetry when you come across it; and no doubt you will easily distinguish between his three poetical manners, —that in which he shakes the dewdrops from his wing, that in which he carries wildflowers on his wavelets, and that in which he casts up pearls as he rolls. I declare, I can liken such writing to nothing but the orgies in which the evil genii may be supposed to have indulged when they heard of the death of Solomon. The great critic of our land and time is dead, and the uncritical spirit of the English nation proceeds to execute this dance of freedom over his grave. He spent a lifetime trying to teach his countrymen how to use their minds, and the breath is hardly out of his body before the sow that was washed returns with majestic determination to her wallowing in the mire.

I can find no better words in which to speak of the loss of Arnold than those which were used by Gerard Hamilton at the death of Johnson. 'He has made a chasm which not only nothing can fill up, but which nothing has a tendency to fill up. Johnson is dead. Let us go to the next best: there is nobody; no man can be said to put you in mind of Johnson.' I will not compare Arnold with the mob of gentlemen who produce criticism ('quales ego vel Cluvienus'), such woful stuff as I or Lord Coleridge write: I will compare him with the best. He leaves men behind him to whom we cannot refuse the name of critic; but then we need to find some other name for him and to call him more than a critic, as John the Baptist was called more than a prophet. I go to Mr Leslie Stephen, and I am always instructed, though I may not be charmed. I go to Mr Walter Pater, and I am always charmed, though I may not be instructed. But Arnold was not merely instructive or charming nor both together: he was what it seems to me no one else is: he was illuminating.

NOTES

PREFACE

1 In *The Bromsgrovian: Housman Memorial Supplement*, 1936 (published in book form by Henry Holt, New York, 1937), and the appendixes to Grant Richards, *Housman, 1897–1936* (Oxford University Press, 1941). See also 'A. E. Housman: a Controversy' in Cyril Connolly, *The Condemned Playground* (Routledge, 1945), p. 47.

2 *A.E.H. Some Poems, Some Letters and a Personal Memoir by his brother Laurence Housman* (Cape, 1937).

3 *Housman, 1897–1936* by Grant Richards with an introduction by Mrs E. W. Symons and Appendices by G. B. A. Fletcher and Others (Oxford University Press, 1941).

4 See below, p. 15.

5 *A. E. Housman. A Sketch, together with a List of his Writings and Indexes to his Classical Papers*, by A. S. F. Gow, Fellow of Trinity College, Cambridge (Cambridge University Press, 1936). Hereafter cited as Gow.

6 This had been printed, for private distribution only, in 1892 and again in 1933 (see introduction to Section I).

7 Gow, p. 25.

8 *Ibid.* p. 21.

FROM THE PREFACES

1 *M. Manilii Astronomicon Liber Primus.* Recensuit et enarravit A. E. Housman (Londinii, apud Grant Richards, MDCCCCIII). Reprinted, Cambridge University Press, 1937, with *Addenda*, whence five minor corrections have been here incorporated.

2 *Liber Quintus* (Londinii, apud societatem The Richards Press, MDCCCCXXX).

3 *D. Iunii Iuvenalis Saturae.* Editorum in usum edidit A. E. Housman (Londinii, apud E. Grant Richards, MDCCCCV). Reprinted, Cambridge University Press, 1931 and later, with corrections (here incorporated).

REVIEWS, CLASSICAL PAPERS AND LETTERS TO THE PRESS

1 *The Classical Review*, IV (1890), 105.

2 *The Journal of Philology*, XXI (1892), 103 ff.; and XXII (1894), 128. For Housman's early addiction to Propertius see Gow, p. 12.

3 *The Classical Review*, VIII (1894), 251. This review is here printed in full.

4   *The Classical Review*, IX (1895), 22.
5   *Ibid.* XIII (1899), 172.
6   *Ibid.* XIV (1900), 232.
7   *Ibid.* XV (1901), 130.
8   *Ibid.* XVI (1902), 339.
9   *Ibid.* XVIII (1904), 227.
10 *Ibid.* XIX (1905), 121.
11 *Ibid.* XIX (1905), 317.
12 *The Classical Quarterly*, I (1907), 53.
13 *The Cambridge Review* (27 January 1915), p. 160. Printed in full.
14 *Ibid.* (23 May 1917), p. 358. Printed in full.
15 *The Classical Review*, XXXIV (1920), 110. Printed in full. Although published only in 1919, posthumously, this was Bywater's inaugural lecture as Regius Professor of Greek at Oxford, delivered in 1894. R. W. Chapman, in his famous sketch of Bywater, *The Portrait of a Scholar*, published in the same year as this review, averred that 'our scholar knew the history of classical learning as it is unlikely it will ever be known again'. Let readers judge.
16 *The Cambridge Review* (25 May 1923), p. 379. Printed in full.
17 *The Times Literary Supplement* (8 May 1924), p. 286.
18 *The Sunday Times* (23 December 1934).

THE APPLICATION OF THOUGHT TO TEXTUAL CRITICISM

1   *Proceedings of the Classical Association*, XVIII (1922), pp. 67 ff.

BIOGRAPHICAL

1   *The Cambridge Review* (28 November 1919).
2   *Nine Essays*, by Arthur Platt, with a preface by A. E. Housman (Cambridge University Press, 1927).

CEREMONIAL

1   Printed privately, 1913, reprinted in J. R. M. Butler, *Henry Montagu Butler, A Memoir* (1925), p. 193.
2   Printed privately, 1919, reprinted in R. St J. Parry, *Henry Jackson* (1926), p. 115.
3   Printed privately, 1921, for the sponsors of the Frazer Lectureship in Social Anthropology in the Universities of Oxford, Cambridge, Glasgow and Liverpool.
4   Printed privately, 1925, reprinted in the *Cambridge University Reporter* (22 December 1925).
5   Printed privately, 1935, reprinted in the *Cambridge University Reporter* (14 May 1935).

THE NAME AND NATURE OF POETRY

1 First published in May, 1933, by the Cambridge University Press. The third quotation from Shakespeare on p. 189 was given inaccurately in the early impressions: Housman corrected it in his own copy of the first.

APPENDIX

1 From a typescript among the papers of Mrs E. W. Symons, Housman's sister. See Gow, p. 21, and p. xv above. Since Walter Pater, here called Mr, died 30 July 1894, this paper was presumably composed between Housman's arrival at University College London (autumn 1892) and that date. He gave it again 18 January 1901 (and perhaps at other times).

¶ For further details see Gow's list of Housman's writings and indexes to his classical papers; also John Carter and John Sparrow, *A. E. Housman, an annotated hand-list* (London, Hart-Davis, 1952).

¶ The text has been printed from the editions or periodicals specified above. When Housman in 1933 gave permission for the reprint of his *Introductory Lecture* he ended his letter 'I hope the proof-reading will be careful: the Cambridge Press cannot be trusted implicitly'. The Press has been, I doubt not, as conscious as I that we are serving the man who laid it down that 'accuracy is a duty and not a virtue'. But any vigilant readers who may be good enough to draw our attention either to misprints or to infidelities to the copy are hereby advised, first, that minor variations of typographical detail have been accommodated to the style in current use at Cambridge; secondly, that two minor misquotations by A.E.H. from *The Cambridge History of English Literature* have been corrected on p. 117; thirdly that a correction made by A.E.H. in his own copy of Platt's *Essays* has been incorporated on p. 155; and fourthly that I have inserted, in places where I think they must have gone astray, three commas in III 2, two in III 4 and one apiece in III 3 and III 12, and an indefinite article in III 14; and have deleted (following Gow) a definite article in III 5: making nine temerities in all.

¶ Among readers and reviewers who called attention to misprints and other errors in the first impression of this book (now corrected) my debt to Mr E. M. Trehern is paramount.

INDEX

Only the most significant names have been indexed.